P9-EEJ-048

Customer Service

Career Success through Customer Satisfaction

GREENVILLE TECHNICAL COLLEGE
MARKETING DEPARTMENT
P. O. BOX 5616
GREENVILLE, SC 29606-5616

Customer Service

Career Success through Customer Satisfaction

SECOND EDITION

PAUL R. TIMM

The Marriott School of Management
Brigham Young University

Upper Saddle River, NJ 07458

Library of Congress Cataloging-in-Publication Data
Timm, Paul R.
Customer service : career success through customer satisfaction, 2nd ed. / Paul R. Timm.
p. cm.
Includes bibliographical references and index.
ISBN 0-13-085959-1 (pbk.)
1. Customer services. 2. Consumer satisfaction. 3. Customer relations. 4. Success in business. I. Title.
KF320.L4G66 2001
340´.023´73 dc21 00-21870
CIP

Acquisitions Editor: Elizabeth Sugg
Production Liaison: Eileen M. O'Sullivan
Director of Manufacturing and Production: Bruce Johnson
Managing Editor: Mary Carnis
Manufacturing Manager: Ed O'Dougherty
Marketing Manager: Shannon Simonsen
Editorial Assistant: Delia Uherec
Senior Design Coordinator: Miguel Ortiz
Interior Design: Inkwell Publishing Services
Composition: Inkwell Publishing Services
Printing and Binding: R.R. Donnelley Harrisonburg

Prentice-Hall International (UK) Limited, *London*
Prentice-Hall of Australia Pty. Limited, *Sydney*
Prentice-Hall Canada Inc., *Toronto*
Prentice-Hall Hispanoamericana, S.A., *Mexico*
Prentice-Hall of India Private Limited, *New Delhi*
Prentice-Hall of Japan, Inc., *Tokyo*
Prentice-Hall Singapore Pte. Ltd.
Editora Prentice-Hall do Brasil, Ltda., *Rio de Janeiro*

Copyright © 2001, 1998 by Prentice-Hall, Inc., Upper Saddle River, New Jersey 07458. All rights reserved. Printed in the United States of America. This publication is protected by Copyright and permission should be obtained from the publisher prior to any prohibited reproduction, storage in a retrieval system, or transmission in any form or by any means, electronic, mechanical, photocopying, recording, or likewise. For information regarding permission(s) write to: Rights and Permissions Department.

10 9 8 7 6
ISBN 0-13-085959-1

Contents

Preface

I wrote this book in response to a need for a different approach to learning the skills needed to succeed in the challenging arena of customer service.

The other customer service books displayed in bookstores everywhere typically take one of two forms: They either tell the story of one company's efforts at boosting service quality, or they reveal a series of tips and ideas. These are fine as far as they go. I have written several such books myself. And books like this can have value so long as the reader effectively translates the ideas into application for his or her organization. But these books seldom show how to apply these diverse ideas to your organization.

The few textbooks available in customer service tend to offer oversimplified suggestions on how to phrase conversations, how to smile and be polite with customers, and the like. Their simplicity defies the real world where real people don't speak from scripts and real human relationships are complex and ever-changing.

This book takes a different approach. It ties together the best information from bookstore trade books and school textbooks—and then adds more. In this book you will find a clear and usable process for developing the kinds of skills, attitudes, and thinking patterns needed to win customer satisfaction and loyalty. The process includes developing

- a heightened awareness of the challenges and opportunities,
- the tools for dealing with unhappy customers by using the power of customer expectations and by creating loyalty,
- the ability to lead, expand, and empower the service process,
- specific skills for professional success, and
- a clear understanding of the future directions of customer service.

Perhaps no arena offers as much opportunity for organizational and professional success as customer service. It lies at the heart of any organization's reason to exist. The companies that do it well experience enormous profitability, marketplace acceptance, and genuine satisfaction among their employees.

Apply *Customer Service* and enjoy the rewards of professional excellence. Then, let me know how you applied the ideas. I can be reached at e-mail: DrTimm@AOL.com.

ACKNOWLEDGMENTS

The author and editor would like to thank the following commentators for their expert reviews: Garland Keesling, Towson State University; Shek True, Fort Lewis College.

Paul R. Timm, Ph.D.
March 2000

Customer Service

Career Success through
Customer Satisfaction

Foundation Skill 1

Fostering Positive Attitudes

Recognize the Role of Customer Service in Your Success

Great service is about attitude. And a service attitude leads to a richer quality of life, not only in the commercial sector.

—Leonard Berry[1]

WHAT YOU'LL LEARN IN THIS CHAPTER

- No business or individual can succeed without developing the skills that create customer loyalty.
- Although customers may be called by many names, all are engaged in an exchange of value. Some customer exchanges are more intimate and complex than others. Service skills allow you to move customers toward deeper relationships and increased loyalty.
- Advertising is a less cost-effective way of getting new customers than a word-of-mouth recommendation from an existing satisfied customer.
- The cost of lost customers can be many times the simple loss of revenue from what they no longer buy. Ripple effects expand the loss dramatically.

- Virtually all companies *say* the customer's satisfaction is paramount, but few successfully translate good intentions into a workable strategy or the systematic application of useful behaviors.
- Service skills provide a master key to career and personal success. A commitment to such skill development pays enormous dividends.

The Way It Is

No One Succeeds without Providing Customer Service

Customer satisfaction horror stories are everywhere. We've all come to expect less than optimal service despite the claims that we live in a service economy. It is tempting to join the chorus of complainers and no one will criticize you if you do. But we can also look at this state of affairs from another viewpoint: as an opportunity. The upside potential for those who give good service is unlimited. By making the process of customer satisfaction a part of our daily lives, we can virtually guarantee our professional and career success. A key foundation skill needed for this is to foster positive attitudes and an optimistic outlook.

No business or organization can succeed without building customer satisfaction and loyalty. Likewise, no person can make a good living without meeting the needs of customers.

Those statements may seem to be rather broad generalizations, but let's consider the argument a bit further. Most people would agree that a business needs customers—but not everyone works in business. What about other kinds of organizations? Does a government agency need customer satisfaction to succeed? Does a civic organization, church congregation, political party, family, service club, school, or fraternity need satisfied customers to succeed?

To answer these questions, we need first to define what we mean by a customer. The common perception is that a customer is someone who buys something from you. Most people assume that to buy involves the exchange of money. True enough. But a broader view of "customer" may be more useful. In its broadest sense *a customer is someone with whom we exchange value.*

> A "customer" can be broadly defined as any person with whom we exchange value.

RECOGNIZE ALL THE PLAYERS: CUSTOMERS BY ANY OTHER NAME . . .

We have a lot of names for customers, often varying by the nature of our business or organization. Some examples are clients, patients, passengers, patrons, members, associates, users, buyers, subscribers, readers, viewers, purchasers, end-users, patrons, guests, or cases.

The commonality in all these customers is that they engage in some sort of transaction with us or our organization. They give us something (often, but not always, money) in exchange for something of value (usually services or goods).

Different names for customers can imply different kinds of transactions.

STRIVE TO CREATE CUSTOMER PARTNERSHIPS

Relationships with customers can evolve into rich and fulfilling partnerships. Consultant–author Chip Bell contends that such a customer partnership arises from certain attitudes or orientations. He says that such partnerships are

- anchored in an attitude of generosity—a "giver" perspective that finds pleasure in extending the relationship beyond just meeting a need or requirement;
- grounded in trust;
- bolstered by a joint purpose;
- marked by truth, candor, and straight talk mixed with compassion and care;
- based on balance, pursuit of equality (more about this in Chapter 4);
- grounded in grace, which Bell describes as "an artistic flow that gives participants a sense of familiarity and ease."[2]

Not every customer relationship becomes a partnership, of course. But such partnerships represent the highest level of customer–provider affiliation.

The customer partnership reflects a high-level relationship.

Notwithstanding the semantic distinctions about customers, it remains useful to agree that everyone has customers; we interact with people who depend on us to provide them with information, guidance, services, products, or social support—in short, value. In exchange for this value, we give something back. This exchange system defines, on the most basic level, what it means to be a customer. When this exchange evolves into something

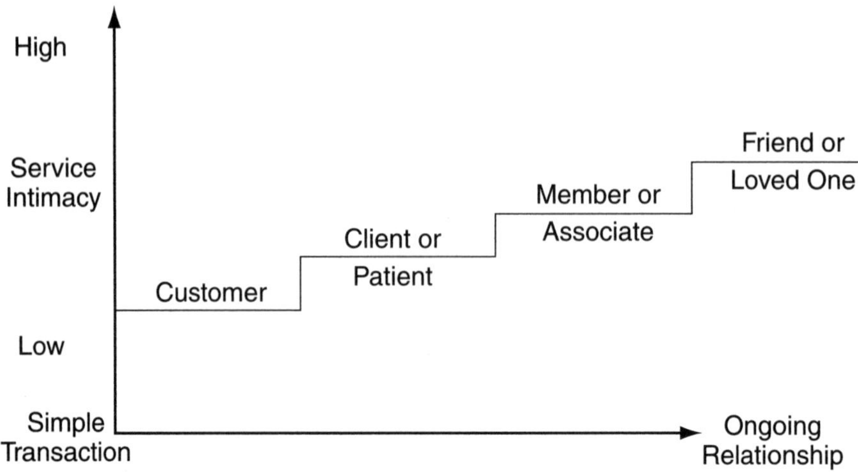

Figure 1-1 Levels of "Customer" Relationships

more—when we move up the steps of relationship building—we enjoy immense levels of career and personal satisfaction.

MAKE THE MOST OF SOCIAL EXCHANGES

Let's get back to basics for a moment. As human beings we are constantly exchanging value with each other. We are, by nature, social beings. We give and take from one another. When we exchange money for a product or service, we are customers. When we provide work in exchange for a wage, our boss and our company are our customers. When we participate in a civic organization or church group, the people to whom we give support, advice, ideas, information, and the like are our customers. When we give of ourselves to contribute to a strong family, our spouse, parents, kids, and other family members become our customers. When we build and maintain networks of friends and associates, we become each others' customers.

By accepting this broader view of what it means to be and have customers, we will see that applying the principles of customer service results in much more than business or financial success. Customer service is a key to career success, but more importantly, it is a master key to success in all phases of one's life. By applying the customer service principles in this book to every aspect of your life, you will gain exceptional levels of success and life satisfaction.

> The broader view of the term customer reminds us that customer service skills can be widely applied to all aspects of life.

Customer service skill is the master key to success.

Customer service skills—the ability to create value—are easy to develop and apply. Your success depends largely on your attitude and a willingness to try new behaviors.

GET AND KEEP CUSTOMERS

New customers can be tough to get. An oft-quoted statistic says that it costs five or six times more to get a new customer than to keep an existing one. So it makes sense to focus on satisfying customers you already have, thus encouraging repeat business. Barring that, you'll spend a lot of time and effort refilling a leaky bucket as you chase an ever diminishing supply of new customers. (This is the dilemma faced by companies that offer shoddy products. People may buy from them one time but will not come back.)

Getting new customers and replacing lost ones is an expensive part of any business.

Some people think that advertising is a good way to induce people to buy. In fact, U.S. businesses spend about $11.5 billion a year on advertising. Yet a recent survey showed that only 25 percent of those polled said that a television ad would induce them to buy. Likewise only 15 percent and 13 percent, respectively, said that newspaper or magazine ads caused them to buy. In short, traditional advertising has little confidence among consumers. Advice or the recommendation from a friend or relative, however, scored 63 percent as a determinant of people's buying a new product.[3] This confirms what people have long known: Word of mouth is still the best way to attract customers.

To sustain repeat business, a business has to generate positive word-of-mouth "advertising" with great service. People talk to others about a service experience when it is exceptional, out of the ordinary. You can have the best products available, but if you fail to supplement them with a positive service experience, few people will notice the difference between you and your competition. Service success is a matter of setting yourself apart from other sources of products through unexpected excellence.

Advertising is less effective at getting customers than positive word of mouth.

RECOGNIZE THE GOOD NEWS AND BAD NEWS . . .

Across the economy, organizational results with customers offer both good and bad news—both pain and opportunity.

First the bad news: The average American company will lose 10 percent to 30 percent of its customers this year, mostly because of poor service. When customers have a choice, they will go to the competition up to one-third of the time. Customer satisfaction is like an election held every day, and the people vote with their feet. If dissatisfied, they walk (sometimes run) to your competitor. When customers don't have a choice—such as in dealing with public utilities or government agencies—they'll use their feet for something else: They'll kick back.

> Customer service is like a daily election, and customers vote with their feet.

Now the good news: Organizations that initiate effective customer-retention programs have seen profits jump 25 to 100 percent. Nonprofit groups see reduced turnover, better financial results, and happier staffs. Like it or not, customer service will always be the decisive battleground where winners and losers are quickly sorted out.

CALCULATE THE TERRIBLE COST OF THE LOST CUSTOMER

What happens when we give poor service and the customer "walks"? Most people don't understand the real cost of a lost customer. When an unhappy customer decides to stop doing business with us, the costs are much more than we realize.

To get a clearer view of the cost impact of a lost customer, let's consider a business we are all familiar with: a grocery supermarket. Here's a story of Mrs. Williams:[4]

> Harriet Williams, a sixty-something single woman, has been shopping at Happy Jack's Super Market for many years. The store is close to home and its products competitively priced. Last week, Mrs. Williams approached the produce manager and said, "Sonny, can I get a half head of lettuce?" He looked at her like she was crazy and curtly said, "Sorry, lady. We just sell the whole head." She was a bit embarrassed but accepted his refusal.

> Later she had several other small disappointments (she wanted a quart of skim milk and they only had half-gallons), and when she checked out her groceries she was largely ignored by the clerk, who was carrying on a conversation with a fellow employee. The clerk made matters worse by abruptly demanding "two forms of ID" with Harriet's check ("What do they think I am, a common criminal?") and failing to say thank you.

Mrs. Williams stepped out of the store that day and decided that she was no longer going to do business there. Although she had shopped at Happy Jack's for many years, she realized that she had never felt that her business was appreciated. She got the overall feeling that Happy Jack's employees couldn't care less if she shopped there. She spent about fifty hard-earned dollars there every week, but to the store employees she was just another cash cow to be milked without so much as a sincere "thank you." Nobody seemed to care whether she was a satisfied customer. But today is different—no more "nice" Mrs. Williams! Today she decided to buy her groceries elsewhere. Maybe—just maybe—there is a store where they'll appreciate her business.

Goodbye, Mrs. Williams.

What do the employees think about that? They're not worried. Life is like that. You win some; you lose some. Happy Jack's is a pretty big chain and doesn't really need Mrs. Williams. Besides, she can be a bit cranky at times and her special requests are stupid. (Who ever heard of buying a half head of lettuce!) They'll survive without her $50 a week. Too bad she's unhappy, but a big company like this can't twist itself into contortions just to save one little old lady from going down the street to the competition.

Sure, we believe in treating customers well, but we're businesspeople. Let's look at the bottom line. After all, it can hardly be considered a major financial disaster to lose a customer like Mrs. Williams. Or can it?

APPRECIATE THE COST OF THE LOST

The employees at Happy Jack's need to understand some economic facts of life. Successful businesses look long term. They look at the "ripple effects" of their service, not just at the immediate profit from an individual purchase.

The shortsighted employee sees Mrs. Williams as a small customer dealing with a big company. Let's change that view: Look at the situation from another, broader perspective.

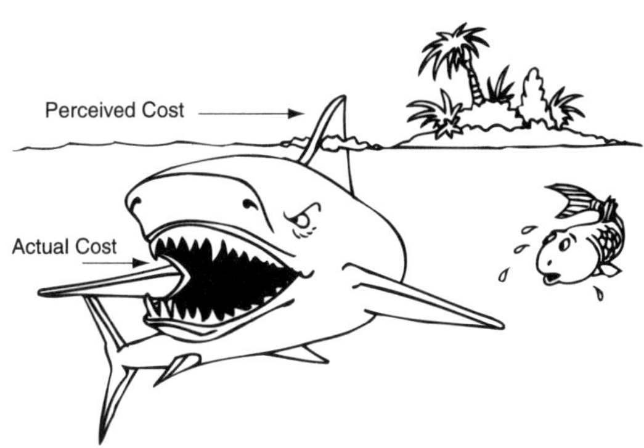

Ho, Hum, Just the Loss of One Small Customer . . .or Is It?

The loss of Mrs. Williams is not, of course, a $50 loss. It's much, much more. She was a $50-a-week buyer. That's $2,600 a year or $26,000 over a decade. Perhaps she would shop at Happy Jack's for a lifetime, but we'll use the more conservative 10-year figure for illustration.

But the ripple effects make it much worse. Studies show that *an upset customer tells on average between 10 and 20 other people about an unhappy experience.* Some people will tell many more, but let's stay conservative and assume that Mrs. Williams told 11. The same studies say that these 11 *may tell an average of 5 others each.* This could be getting serious!

Upset customers tell other people.

How many people are likely to hear the bad news about Happy Jack's? Look at the math:

Mrs. Williams	1 person
tells eleven others	+11 people
who tell five each	+55 people
for a total who heard of	67 people

Are all 67 of these people going to rebel against Happy Jacks? Probably not. Let's assume that of these 67 customers or potential customers, only one-quarter of them decide not to shop at Happy Jack's. Twenty-five percent of 67 (rounded) is 17.

Assuming that these 17 people would also be $50-a-week shoppers, Happy Jack's stands to lose $44,200 a year, or $442,000 in a decade because Mrs. Williams was upset when she left the store. Somehow giving her that half a head of lettuce doesn't sound so stupid.

Although these numbers are starting to get alarming, they are still conservative. In many parts of the country, a typical supermarket customer actually spends about $100 a week; so losing another customer could quickly double these figures.

How Much Will It Cost to Replace These Customers?

Customer service research says that *it costs about five to six times more to attract a new customer* (mostly advertising and promotion costs) *than it does to keep an existing one* (where costs may include giving

Replacing lost customers is extremely costly.

refunds, offering samples, replacing merchandise, or giving half a head of lettuce). One report put these figures at about $19 to keep a customer happy versus $118 to get a new buyer into the store.

Again, some quick math shows the real cost of the lost Mrs. Williams:

- Cost of keeping Mrs. Williams happy = $ 19
- Cost of attracting 17 new customers = $2006

Now let's make our economic "facts of life" even more meaningful to each employee.

UNDERSTAND HOW LOST CUSTOMERS MEAN LOST JOBS

The Robert Half Organization, a well-known personnel consulting firm, shows a simple way to calculate the amount of sales needed to pay employee salaries. Assuming that a company pays 50 percent in taxes and earns a profit of 5 percent after taxes, Table 1-1 shows how much must be sold to pay each employee (in three different salary levels) and maintain current profit levels:

Table 1-1 Sales Needed to Sustain a Job

Salary	Benefits	After-Tax Cost	Sales Needed
$25,000	$11,500	$18,250	$365,000
$15,000	$ 6,900	$10,950	$219,000
$10,000	$ 4,600	$ 7,300	$146,000

These figures will vary, of course. But the impact on one's job can be clearly shown.

If a $10,000-a-year part-time clerk irritates as few as three or four customers in a year, the ripple effects can quickly exceed the amount of sales needed to maintain that job! Unfortunately, many organizations have employees who irritate three or four customers a day! Ouch.

RECOGNIZE THE MYTHS: THE CUSTOMER IS ALWAYS RIGHT AND OTHER BALONEY

Most people accept, or at least give lip service to, the idea that "the customer is the boss," that he or she is a king or queen (or at least a prince or princess!). They talk about the customer always being right. They say that the customer is "our reason for existing" as an organization, *ad nauseam.*

Self-Analysis

Applying the Mrs. Williams Example to Your Company

Let's take a few moments and go back to the Mrs. Williams example, but instead use your own organization. Suppose that you lose one customer and the other statistics hold true. Take a few moments to calculate the numbers as they apply to your organization. If you work for a nonprofit or government agency where dollar sales are not a relevant measure, calculate the number of people who may be aggravated or upset with you and your organization. Think in terms of the psychological price that must be paid as you deal with frustrated, angry, or upset patrons on a day-to-day basis.

Calculating the Cost of Your Lost Customer*

A. Average or typical dollar amount spent (per week or month as appropriate):		\$_____ per (customer)
B. Annual dollar amount (weekly figure × 52 or monthly figure × 12):		\$_______
C. Decade dollar amount (B × 10):		\$_______
D. Ripple effect costs (B × 17—people who may follow an unhappy customer out the door):	+	\$_______
Annual revenue lost:	=	\$_______
Then,		
E. Add customer replacement costs of 17 customers × \$118 (a typical figure):	=	\$2,006.00
F. Minus the cost of keeping your present customer happy (\$19 is a typical figure):	–	\$ 19.00
G. "Replacement" costs (E – F):	=	\$1,987.00
Finally,		
Total the revenue lost figures (B or C + G)		
A rough cost of your lost:		\$_______

*Note: These calculations are designed only to get you thinking about the ripple effects of unhappy customers. Their mathematical precision is not guaranteed nor is it important. The point is that lost customers cost a lot of money.

One of the greatest challenges lies in translating slogans or good intentions into behaviors customers want.

Yet despite these claims, how is the service? Often, not great.

The real challenge lies in translating such slogans into actions that convey these feelings and beliefs *to the customer.* Even when leaders truly believe in the importance of customer service, they still face the difficulty of getting the customer contact people to do what customers want—even when the customer's request may be a bit unusual. The problem gets trickier when you realize that the lowest-paid and least-trained employees are often those who face the customer every day.

- A multimillion-dollar fast-food restaurant, for example, places its success squarely in the hands of the minimum-wage teenager taking the orders and delivering the food.
- The image of a huge financial institution is created in the minds of customers by the entry-level teller who handles their day-to-day transactions.
- A multibillion-dollar government agency is judged largely by the receptionist who answers the phone or greets the customer, thus setting a tone for any transaction. (Many a criticism of the "government bureaucracy" can be traced to a receptionist "getting off on the wrong foot" with a patron.)

When you really buy into the value of the customer and somehow communicate that to each customer, you virtually guarantee your success. When you supervise others, you need to "infect" them with your same positive attitudes and skills. That can be a challenge for leaders, something we'll talk more about in Chapter 6.

KNOW WHY SERVICE IS IMPORTANT TO YOU—YES, YOU!

Businesses benefit from good service, but suppose you don't own a business. As "just an employee," what can you gain from developing service skills?

The short answer is that customer service skills are the same skills that bring success and satisfaction to all aspects of life. The best reason for learning the process of customer satisfaction is that *it makes you feel better about your life and yourself.* Sure, there are solid business reasons as we've already discussed. But ultimately the personal advantage can be even greater.

Service skills are crucial for success at all organizational levels.

Based on 30 years of business and professional experience in a variety of organizations, I am absolutely certain that people who apply the kinds of skills discussed in this book are happier, more productive, more successful and, yes, wealthier than people who choose to ignore the power of customer service. Take that statement on faith for now, but as you study and apply the ideas in the remaining chapters of this book, you will see what I mean.

We all start out as "peons" in organizations. Yet from day one, we choose how much we want to give to that organization. The more we give, the more we get. That's a principle of life that has been proven true throughout time. The flip side—giving the least we can get away with—is simply unacceptable. Giving average or substandard service is hazardous to your career health. Undistinguished service leads to extinguished customers.

A commitment to using customer service skills ignites a growth process.

The person who makes a commitment to mastering the process of customer service will be light-years ahead of one who fails to do so. Betsy Sanders, a Nordstrom retail executive, says, "The nature of such a [personal] commitment is perhaps best represented by a helix, which curves back around on itself but always moves up as it comes around. Thus, wherever you are in the process, the principles of service leadership provided can be applied to your situation now and will also support your ongoing development."[5]

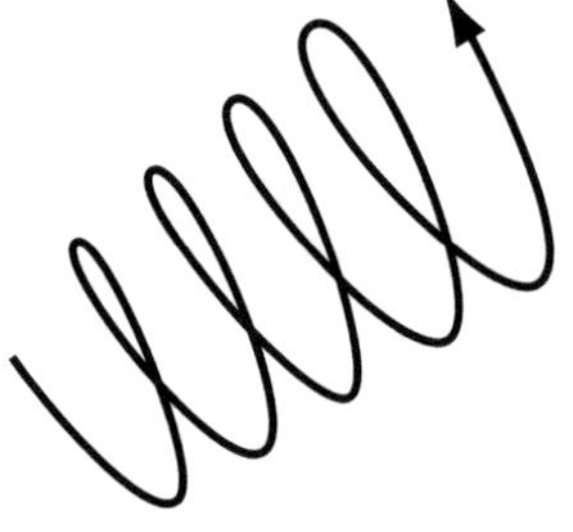

The Customer Service Helix

Service Snapshot

Burgers Supreme

Steve and Debby K. own an independent fast-food restaurant called Burgers Supreme. For more than six years they have built up a loyal clientele, many of whom eat there almost every day. Not only do their customers buy lunch at Burgers Supreme, but they bring in friends and fellow workers. Some of the regulars are teased about obviously owning stock in the restaurant, although none do.

The menu is broad, covering dozens of sandwiches, salads, soups, desserts, and specialty foods like gyros, onion rings, and frozen yogurt. Everything is prepared fresh. But the loyalty goes far beyond good food and fair prices.

Almost every regular customer has had the unexpected surprise of having Steve, Debby, or one of their employees say, "This meal's on me" and refusing to accept a dime. Obviously this doesn't happen every time you go in, but it does reflect the owner's way of recognizing customer loyalty. It also reflects their willingness to empower their employees to give something away now and then.

The counter help at Burgers Supreme learns from Debby's example to greet customers by name, smile, cheerfully fix any mistakes, and keep hustling to make sure the restaurant is clean, even during the busiest lunch hour.

Faced with tremendous competition from national chains like Wendy's, McDonald's, and others (who serve similar fare), Burgers Supreme "eats their lunch," so to speak, with friendly, individual, personalized service. They don't just talk the talk of customer service. They walk the walk.

STRIVE FOR THE ULTIMATE GOAL: CUSTOMERS FOR LIFE

The ultimate goal of customer service is to create customer loyalty. Understanding loyalty—what makes your customer loyal and how to measure this—enables a company or person to improve customer-driven service quality. We'll talk more about this later in the book, but for now, it is important to understand what loyalty means.[6]

Define Customer Loyalty

To best understand customer loyalty, first recognize what it is not. Customer loyalty is sometimes mistaken for:

> Some customer behaviors may create the image of loyalty, but can be counterfeit.

- Customer satisfaction alone. Satisfaction is a necessary component but a customer may be satisfied today yet not necessarily loyal to you in the future.
- A response to some trial offer or special incentive. You can't buy loyalty, you must earn it.
- A large share of the market. You may have a large percentage of the customers for a particular product or service for reasons other than customer loyalty. Perhaps your competitors are poor or your current prices more attractive.
- Repeat buying alone. Some people buy as a result of habit, convenience, or price but would be quick to defect to an alternative.

Recognizing counterfeit loyalty is important. It can lull you into a false sense of security while your competition may be building real customer loyalty. A more reliable definition of loyalty is a composite of three important characteristics:

1. It is driven by *overall satisfaction.* Low or erratic levels of satisfaction disqualify the company from earning customer loyalty.
2. It involves a commitment on the part of the customer to make a sustained *investment in an ongoing relationship* with a company.
3. It is reflected by a combination of attitudes and behaviors including:
   - *repeat buying* (or the intention to do so as needed),
   - *a willingness to recommend* the company to others, and
   - a commitment to the company demonstrated by a *resistance to switch* to a competitor.

We'll talk more about customer loyalty throughout the book, including how to develop a customer loyalty index in Chapter 5. For now, let's agree that customer loyalty is the highest goal of our service efforts.

> True customer loyalty is a function of overall satisfaction, willingness to strengthen the relationship, repeat buying, and willingness to recommend you to others.

Another Look

A Great Harvest![7]

While most company owners say that word-of-mouth marketing is important to their business, few take it as seriously as Janene Centurione, who operates two Great Harvest Bread bakeries, in Ann Arbor and Birmingham, Michigan. The $2.2-million business turns loyal customers into experts, enlisting them to spread the word about the company's gourmet bread.

Centurione and her 50 employees look for enthusiastic patrons who ask lots of questions about the bread and pastry products. Employees then ask those customers to sign a guest book, which automatically initiates them into a "bread zealot" club.

Aside from funds for an occasional newspaper advertisement, virtually all of Centurione's marketing budget is used to inform and reward special customers. Each month she sends out postcards to almost 7,000 people (about 20 percent of her clientele) that share information, like bread recipes. Zealots receive early notices about new product releases, along with the occasional 10 percent–off coupon. Some postcards thank customers for their referrals, which Centurione knows they're making, since the only place she mentions her latest breads is on the postcards, and the majority of orders come from people who say they heard about them from a friend.

Centurione estimates that the annual cost of keeping customers in the know comes to about $7 a head and that each recruit to the club brings in about $200 a year. She contrasts that with the $80 a year she spent on bringing in each new customer when she relied solely on traditional advertising. In two years, per-visit sales have climbed from $4.75 to $8.75, which she believes is directly attributable to an increased awareness of her products. Simultaneously, net sales have grown 18 percent a year for the past three years, while the number of zealots has increased almost tenfold.

Probes

1. Why do you think these customers become "enthusiastic patrons"?
2. How could your business apply a process like this to build customer loyalty?

A FINAL THOUGHT

Customer service skill development provides the most significant arena for career success. Whether you work for a huge corporation or run a lemonade stand, the principles of customer service remain the same. You live and die by what your customers think of you.

In fact, *your number-one task,* regardless of your job title, organizational position, experience, or seniority, will *always* be to attract, satisfy, and preserve loyal customers.

Summary of Key Ideas

- No business or individual can succeed without creating customer satisfaction.
- Customers may be called by many names but all are engaged in an exchange of value. Some customer relationships are more intimate and complex, but the exchange element remains constant. Moving customers toward deeper relationships with you requires service skills.
- Advertising is generally less cost-effective in getting new customers than word-of-mouth recommendations from an existing satisfied customer.

- The cost of lost customers can be many times the simple reduction of their sales. Ripple effects expand the loss dramatically.
- While all companies say the customer's satisfaction is paramount, few successfully translate good intentions into a workable strategy or specific behavior.
- Ultimately, service skills provide a master key to career and personal success. A commitment to such skill development pays enormous dividends.

Key Terms and Concepts

Customer	Ripple effects
Customer loyalty	Service skills
Customer partnerships	The cost of the lost customer
Customer service skills	Word-of-mouth advertising

Self-Test Questions

1. What defines a customer?
2. What are some of the attitudes and orientations that define a customer partnership?
3. How can you apply customer service skills to your everyday life?
4. Why do word-of-mouth recommendations work better than advertising for attracting new customers?
5. Why is it important to focus on satisfying your existing customers before worrying about adding new customers?
6. How do ripple effects escalate the cost of one lost customer?
7. What three characteristics define real customer loyalty?
8. What behaviors are sometimes mistaken for customer loyalty, but are not?

Application Activity: Interview Service Providers

1. Interview five people about their customer service attitudes. Specifically, ask them to describe their internal and external customers and what they feel about the importance of serving them.
2. Ask two businesspeople to estimate the typical amount customers spend with them. Then calculate the "cost of the lost" scenario like the one in the chapter. Ask the businessperson to react to this estimate. Does it seem plausible? Too high? Too low?
3. Describe three businesses that have won your customer loyalty—ones you enjoy doing business with and are likely to remain a customer with. What, specifically, causes you to give them your loyalty? (Note: Often subtle things win you over.)

4. What major corporations that you've heard of seem to be doing the best job of building customer loyalty? In what ways do they attempt to build long-term relationships with customers?

Notes

[1]L. Berry, *On Great Service: A Framework for Action,* as quoted in *The Seattle Times,* published via America Online, April 3, 1995.

[2]C. R. Bell, *Customers as Partners* (San Francisco: Berrett-Koehler Publishers, 1994), pp. 5–6.

[3]K. Goldman, "Study Finds Ads Induce Few People to Buy," *Wall Street Journal,* October 17, 1995, p. B6.

[4]I first used this example in my book, *50 Powerful Ideas You Can Use to Keep Your Customers,* 2nd ed. (Hawthorne, NJ: Career Press, 1995), pp. 15–19.

[5]B. Sanders, *Fabled Service* (San Diego, CA: Pfeiffer & Company, 1995), p. xv.

[6]Adapted from a discussion by A. Purs and D. R. Brandt. "Understanding Your Customers," *Marketing Tools,* July/August 1995, pp. 10–11.

[7]S. Schafer, "Informing Customers," *INC Magazine,* June 1996. Transmitted on America Online, June 18, 1996. Reprinted with permission.

Foundation Skill

1

Recognize and Deal with Customer Turnoffs

The Customer Keeps the Score

Research by the Forum Corporation suggests that 70% of the customers lost by 13 big service and manufacturing companies [studied] had scooted because of a lack of attention from the front-line employees. It's an emotional tie, not mere satisfaction that brings the customer back.

—Tom Peters[1]

WHAT YOU'LL LEARN IN THIS CHAPTER

- Everyone has pet peeves about the service they receive. In most case, these irritators are little things.
- The cumulative impact of little customer irritators can be dramatic, as illustrated by the Kmart versus Wal-Mart example.
- Customer turnoffs arise from value, systems, or people problems.
- The value of getting people out of their "zone of indifference" and into the category of loyal customers.
- The two major steps needed to create customer loyalty.
- Five tips for better listening when dealing with customer complaints.

- How to use systematic observation, active listening, explorer groups, mystery shoppers, focus groups, and feedback cards to assess customer satisfaction, expectations, and wants.

The Way It Is

Involve the Customer in Defining Value

A great way for a business to fall on its face is to assume that it knows exactly what the customer wants—without actually asking the customer. In the 1980s and early 1990s Volkswagen Corporation of America saw its sales drop by 90 percent, from its 1970 high of over a half-million cars to less than 50,000 in 1993. What happened?

Much of VW's competitive advantage in subcompact cars evaporated when competitors (especially the Japanese manufacturers) engaged in extended conversations with their customers and used feedback received to develop appealing features. While VW engineers "knew the *right* way" to position a steering wheel, Japanese compacts offered adjustable tilt wheels. While VW was certain that its radios were "just fine," competitors responded to customer desires for multi-speaker stereo sound systems.

The result: Customers perceived VW as offering less value. By the early 1990s Volkswagen of America was fighting for its life. Today it has gone through a dramatic turnaround after having paid a terrible price for not staying current with customer expectations and wants. To stay on top, you've got to involve the customer in defining value.[2]

BE AWARE THAT EVERYONE HAS PET PEEVES ABOUT SERVICE

Get a few people together and ask them to describe some pet peeves about their experiences as customers and you'll get an earful. Everyone can recall situations when they were treated poorly or they received products that just didn't measure up.

I often begin customer service training sessions by having the group generate a list of gripes to get people to think about specifically irritating experiences. You may find it useful to articulate some of your pet peeves. Take a moment to make a list of *specific* things that turn you off when you are a customer.

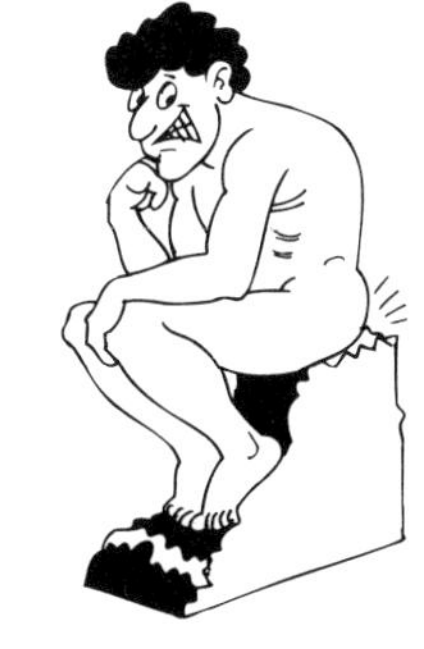

Think about your "pet peeves" about customer service.

Self-Analysis

My Pet Peeves in Customer Service

Quickly list your top ten specific turnoffs. What kinds of things irritate you when you are a customer? Think about several customer contexts: retail, repair services, restaurants, government agencies, etc. Be as specific as possible about exactly what irritates you. Perhaps cite a specific example if that helps you express your idea.

1. NOT HONORING POSTED PRICE
2. EXPLAINING WHY "YOU'RE WRONG" (BEN. OF DOUBT)
3. DIRTY BATHROOMS
4. LONG LINES
5. REQUIRING MORE INFO THAN WHAT'S REALLY NEEDED
6. IMPATIENT BODY LANG.
7. POOR LISTN'G 4 DETAILS
8. BEING OUT OF SALE ITEMS
9. BEING TOO ATTENTIVE
10. POOR ANTICP'N OF NEEDS

A typical list of turnoffs generated in a training workshop includes things like:

- rude or indifferent service,
- having to wait too long,
- poor quality work (especially on repair jobs),
- sale items not in stock,
- dirty restaurants,
- phone calls put on hold,
- employees lacking knowledge,
- high-pressure sales tactics, or
- the employee talking down to me.

> Everyone has examples of irritating experiences as customers.

RECOGNIZE THAT THE LITTLE THINGS MEAN EVERYTHING

Service turnoffs are, more often than not, little things that irritate us. Problems with shoddy products or poor-quality service happen, of course, but little things are most likely to grind us in everyday customer experiences.

We can typically buy almost any product we want from several different vendors. We can buy a television from an upscale department or furniture store, a discount store, an electronics shop, a catalog merchant, a consumer warehouse, or even via the Internet. What causes us to choose one over the other?

> Since most things can be purchased from one of several places, what factors determine where we shop?

Price is a consideration for many consumers, of course, but what if the prices are about the same? In those cases (or for the non-price-sensitive buyer) we are likely to decide on the basis of a lot of little things. Perhaps we like (or strongly dislike) a store's advertising approach. Perhaps the location is convenient, the merchandise displays are attractive, the clerks are friendly and knowledgeable, or the selection and warranty offered are good.

Perhaps the illustration of little things making big differences is no more evident than in the competition among the giant discount retailers. In the 1980s the discount giant Kmart Corporation surpassed Sears to become the world's largest retailer. Kmart's reign at the top was, however, short-lived. In the early 1990s, Wal-Mart passed Kmart for the number one spot. What's the difference between Kmart and Wal-Mart?

> Little things can account for huge competitive advantages.

Think about that question. What is the difference between a Kmart and a Wal-Mart store? You could list a lot of similarities. In fact, Kmart and Wal-Mart stores are similar in size, locations, layouts, colors, display, merchandise sold, prices, and many other characteristics. So what accounted for the stagnant growth of Kmart and the stratospheric rise of Wal-Mart in the mid-1990s?

A good case can be made for the little things Wal-Mart has implemented to improve customer service. In fact, when I ask participants in training sessions to identify things they *expect* from a Wal-Mart that are different from Kmart, they inevitably cite:

- the greeters at the door to welcome customers;
- employees wearing vests with name tags to help customers find things;

- cleaner floors, tidier parking lots, stores that don't smell like popcorn; and
- quick checkouts staffed with friendly people who actually seem to like their jobs.

Notice how I prefaced this list: Identify things they *expect* to be different. As we'll see later in the book, expectations can be more important than the reality. In reality, some Kmart stores do a good job with all these things listed. But customers don't typically expect those things from Kmart.

The results of these kinds of little things are astounding. When Wal-Mart first surpassed Kmart in the early nineties, both retailers had sales of about $34 billion a year. Today the gap has become huge. Kmart continues to sell $30 to $40 billion as I write this. Wal-Mart sells about $160 billion. And they sell the same kinds of stuff for about the same prices via the same number of stores! Little things mean *everything* when it comes to customer loyalty.

Greeters can put a human face on a large company.

© 1997, Washington Post Writers Group. Reprinted with permission.

Service Snapshot

Michelle's Attention to Detail Means PR Firm Success

Minding details projects an attitude of professionalism that attracts and keeps customers. Michelle, who started a public relations business, was explaining her communications techniques to a prospective client when suddenly the company executive interrupted: Could she promise that her work wouldn't be marred with misspellings?

Misspellings? Michelle was stunned. She couldn't imagine why the executive asked. Later client calls revealed a pattern: Inattention to the "little stuff"—not returning phone calls promptly, not itemizing bills, acting before asking for approval—was driving prospective clients wild. "The real key for succeeding in business is not always brilliance but competence in day-to-day details," Michelle says. She won an account once because she was the only presenter who followed up her meeting with a letter.[3]

IDENTIFY THREE CATEGORIES OF CUSTOMER TURNOFFS

To better understand customer turnoffs, I've collected thousands of responses about specific things that irritate people. Some categories became clear as I analyzed the responses with researcher Kristen DeTienne. We found that customer turnoffs fall into three categories: value, systems, and people.[4]

Value Turnoffs

A fundamental turnoff is the feeling among customers that they receive poor value in a product or service received. In short, shoddy products or sloppy work can put customers through the roof.

Value can be simply defined as *quality relative to price paid.* If you purchase an inexpensive, throwaway item at a discount store—say a 79-cent pen—you may not be upset if it doesn't last very long. But buy a $79 fountain pen that leaks in your shirt pocket and you're furious. If you make a major purchase of an automobile, appliance, or professional service, and it quits working or fails to meet your needs, you experience a value turnoff.

> Value is a function of product quality relative to its price.

The major responsibility for providing customers with appropriate value lies with the top leadership of the organization. It's the executive decision makers in a company who determine the products or services that will be sold. Value can also go back to the designers of the products (as in our opening story about Volkswagen). In a one-person enterprise, the owner determines the quality/pricing formula that defines value. If you run a lemonade stand, you determine how many lemons and how much sugar to use. (You should also check with your customers to see how they like it.) Other people in an organization can affect value, but leadership bears the major responsibility for assuring it.

Systems Turnoffs

Say the word "systems" and many people thing of computers. The term *systems*, however, is broader than that. Here it describes any *process, procedure, or policy used to "deliver" the product or service to the customer.* Systems are the way we get the value to the customer. When seen this way, systems include such things as:

- company location, layout, parking facilities, and phone lines;
- employee training and staffing;

- record keeping (including computer systems for handling customer transactions);
- policies regarding guarantees, returns, etc.;
- delivery or pickup services;
- marketing and sales policies;
- customer follow-up procedures.

Systems involve any action or procedure used to get the product or service to a customer. System problems are primarily the responsibility of management.

The elimination of system turnoffs is primarily the responsibility of managers in most organizations. This is because often system changes require spending money (e.g., for new locations, remodeling, additional staffing and training, initiating delivery services, etc.). Nonmanagement employees can and should be involved in suggesting system changes, however. Management can get some of its best change ideas from employees at all levels. (Ways to get ideas from employees are discussed in Chapter 9.)

How Important Are Systems?

Some people argue that the majority of customer service problems are systems-related. Business consultant Michael Gerber believes that systems are the key to business success. He cites hamburger giant McDonald's as an example: Gerber talks about the frustration of small businesspeople who fail to learn this lesson. He describes working with a client named Murray, who was so tied up in the day-to-day work of his business that he failed to grow a successful company. Gerber calls this episode, "The Day I Fell in Love with McDonald's." Here is an excerpt from a brochure advertising Gerber's "The E-Myth Seminar:"[5]

> When my meeting with Murray ended, I was exhausted. I had pages of notes, hours of conversations swirling in my head, and a long drive home. I needed a few minutes to collect my thoughts. So, I pulled into a McDonald's to grab a bite and sort out my notes.
>
> Talk about being confused. I didn't know where to start with Murray and his company. He loved his product and his dreams for the future. But something was wrong. I just couldn't put my finger on it . . . Then it hit me.
>
> Maybe it's fate, but that day was the first time I was in a McDonald's twice in the same day. Suddenly, from the corner of my eye, I watched a lady approach the counter, and the young girl who was serving asked if she could take her order. Nothing out of the ordinary. But there was something about *what* happened that caught my interest. It was both what she said and *her manner* of saying it.
>
> I've been to McDonald's restaurants from coast-to-coast. And I've been served by males and females, young and old, and many different ethnic groups. But regardless of where I am, or who is serving me, two very inter-

esting things happen to me each time. First, I feel *comfortable,* because I know what to expect. And second, because I know what to expect, I feel *in control of my experience.*

At that moment I knew the secret of the McDonald's success. Wow! What an amazing discovery. Instantly I could see that this *secret* can work in *any* business . . . The essence of the secret is *how* they [sell] that's so wonderful. It's their *system* that makes it a success. The key is that they have a system for *everything.* Regardless of who is working on a shift, the entire staff is taught the system. . . . There is no indecision. No confusion. No hesitation. No sour faces. No frustrated looks. Everything works like a well-oiled machine.

Gerber's observations illustrate the importance of effective systems in any business. The systems can create comfort for both employees and customers. Knowing what to do and how to do it comes, of course, from extensive training and careful design of the delivery systems. Failure to do these things results in many customer service turnoffs.

People Turnoffs

People turnoffs are almost always communication problems. Employees who fail to communicate appropriately, both verbally (with words) and nonverbally (without words), can quickly irritate a customer. Some examples of people turnoffs are:

- failure to greet or even smile at a customer,
- inaccurate information given or lack of knowledge conveyed,
- talking to another employee or allowing telephone interruptions while ignoring a customer,
- a rude or uncaring attitude,
- high-pressure sales tactics,
- inappropriate, dirty, or sloppy appearance (of the employee or the work location), and
- any communicated message that causes the customer to feel uncomfortable.

Employees at all organizational levels can and often do create people turnoffs, often unconsciously. In most cases these turnoffs arise because people fail to understand how they come across to others. Everyone interested in having a successful career would be wise to become constant students of communication. Even the most subtle or unconscious behaviors can communicate the wrong messages and result in lost customers.

> Communication turnoffs are often a result of employee ignorance of the kinds of "messages" employees are sending to customers.

People turnoffs occur when customers feel you don't care.
ZIGGY © 1995 ZIGGY AND FRIENDS, INC. Dist. by UNIVERSAL PRESS SYNDICATE.
Reprinted with permission. All rights reserved.

GET YOUR CUSTOMERS BEYOND THE "ZONE OF INDIFFERENCE"

Thinking about customer turnoffs is particularly important when we consider that the correlation between customer satisfaction and repeat business (loyalty) is rather tenuous. Even satisfied customers may be neutral toward their relationship with a business, and the littlest thing can push them over the edge toward dissatisfaction. Service can meet their needs adequately but fail to motivate their continuing loyalty. Just as motivation researcher Friedrick Herzberg et al. discovered long ago, satisfied workers are not necessarily motivated workers.[6] Likewise, satisfied customers cannot be assumed to be motivated repeat customers. A "zone of indifference" exists between the satisfied and the motivated. Things are okay, but there is little to tie the customer to us in the long run.

Actually, customers who are satisfied may be inert, not motivated. Their satisfaction simply means the absence of dissatisfaction, not the motivation to become a repeat customer. A zone of indifference lies between the dissatisfied and the motivated (see Figure 2-1).

The challenge, then, is to get beyond satisfaction to *motivation*. This is best done by responding to customer perceptions and expectations. Let's consider what we can do if we have a customer who is on the dissatisfied side of the continuum—a customer who needs to be recovered.

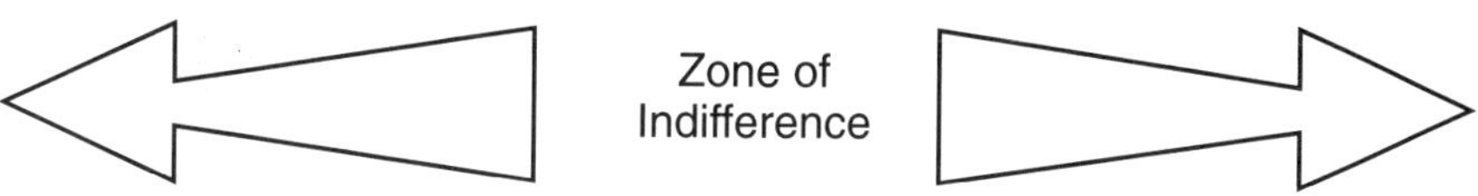

Figure 2-1 The Satisfaction–Motivation Distinction

VALUE SERVICE RECOVERY

Despite the best efforts of customer-savvy people, problems inevitably arise. Problem situations should not be viewed as tragic, but as opportunities to further solidify customer loyalty. Anyone can give good service when customers don't have special needs, but it is precisely when a need or problem arises that customer skills are put to the test.

> Customer problems should be viewed as loyalty-building opportunities.

Chapter 3 goes into detail about how to recover the unhappy customer. For now, you need to know that the payoff for recovering a potentially lost customer is actually an increased likelihood that he or she will be loyal to you, more likely to be motivated according to our model. It sounds strange, but studies have shown that a customer who encounters a problem with a company—and has that problem addressed promptly and effectively—is even more likely to remain loyal than a customer who never had a problem. Ironically, even in cases when the customers' problems are not resolved 100 percent in their favor, loyalty still increases. Just the fact that the problem was acknowledged and addressed seems to be the key variable in strengthening the customer relationship.

> Addressing and attempting to resolve customers' problem earns their loyalty—even if the attempt is not completely successful.

An interesting example of customer recovery occurred when Toyota Motors introduced the Lexus line of luxury cars. With much fanfare, Lexus burst on the scene as *the* standard of excellence in its market. Shortly after the product introduction, it became necessary to recall the vehicles for a design defect. Toyota was embarrassed, of course, but went through with the recall of thousands of new vehicles. But someone in the organization (an optimist, no doubt) saw this recall as an opportunity to showcase the excellent vehicle service Lexus customers would be entitled to. One selling point of the new line of cars was that they would be professionally serviced by exceptional dealers. Various dealers took the opportunity to make lemonade out of this lemon by doing things like:

- calling customers and arranging to pick up their cars so that they wouldn't have to take them to the dealership;
- arranging for loaner cars while the work was done;
- giving every service customer's car a free thorough wash and wax job;
- apologizing and making recompense by giving customers gifts ranging from a fresh rose to a $50 bill to make up for the inconvenience.

In short, Toyota/Lexus turned a potential embarrassment into a watershed opportunity to demonstrate their service excellence. Many Lexus customers cited that experience as the reason they continued to have their cars serviced at the dealerships even after the warranty expired.

LOYALTY COMES FROM CUSTOMER AWARENESS THAT SERVICE *IS* YOUR BUSINESS

Customer loyalty arises from companies that make service an integral part of their operating philosophy. The "service department" should be a redundancy. Every department exists only to serve its customers, internal and external. Nordstrom executive Betsy Sanders says, "As long as you seek to add an extra dynamic to your business [like time, energy, and resources to isolate service as some special program] the results will be disappointing. Service begins to be meaningful when it is an internal dynamic. This dynamic develops when you accept service as the underpinning of your enterprise, believing that without your customers, you would not exist."[7]

> Service must be seen as the very essence of your business, not a side function.

Express gratitude often. Without customers you have no business, no job.

© 1997, Washington Post Writers Group. Reprinted with permission.

Customers are quick to see the depth of a company's commitment to service. The organization that distinguishes itself in the eyes of its customers is rare. Most companies have not made enough of an impression one way or another for their customers to even think about them, much less to share these thoughts with others.[8] That element of loyalty—recommending a company to others—is lost because of undistinguished service.

EARN YOUR CUSTOMERS' LOYALTY

How can we help a customer step outside the zone of indifference and become a "raving fan" of our company? Two steps make sense:

1. Reduce or eliminate value, systems, and people turnoffs.
2. Exceed customer expectations to create a positive awareness.

We'll talk a bit about the first of these in this chapter and go into depth about exceeding expectations in Chapters 4 and 5.

USE THESE SKILLS FOR RECOGNIZING AND ELIMINATING YOUR CUSTOMER'S TURNOFFS

The first step in reducing or eliminating turnoffs is to recognize their existence. The three categories described earlier (value, systems, and people) provide a useful way of categorizing and recognizing who shoulders major responsibility for each. But how can we tell if we are turning off customers?

> There is no substitute for putting yourself in your customer's shoes.

The short answer is to put yourself in the shoes of your customer. Objectively assess the way they are treated and compare this with how other companies may be treating them. As Yogi Berra said, "You can observe a lot by just watching." A systematic way of "watching" is particularly useful because it gives objective data. Five major ways of gathering data include listening, explorer groups, mystery shoppers, focus groups, and feedback forms.

Listen with More Than Your Ears

Few people are really good listeners, but those who are gain a lot of good information. Some people mistakenly think that listening is a passive activity—something you "sit back" and do when you are not talking. Not so. Good listening requires active mental work.

When you do it well, people open up and share important ideas with you.

Good listening requires active mental effort.

Pay attention to your talk/listen ratio. If you talk a lot more than you listen, you could be turning off your customer or failing to get good ideas on how to improve. To be a better listener, use these ideas:

- *Judge the content* of what people are saying, *not the way they are saying it.* Customers may not have the "right" words, but they know what they need better than anyone. Look past their tone of voice or their inability to articulate exactly what they want. Fish for clarification.
- *Hold your fire.* Don't jump to make judgments before your customers finish talking. If they're upset, don't respond defensively. Just hear them.
- *Work at listening.* Maintain eye contact and discipline yourself to listen to what is being said. Tune out those thoughts that get you thinking about something else.
- *Resist distractions and interruptions.* Make the customer the center of your attention.
- *Seek clarification* from customers so that you fully understand their needs. Do this in a nonthreatening way, using sincere, open-ended questions. Don't interrogate, but do ask them to help you understand what they mean, if you are confused. (Often the words "Help me to understand" can be an effective way to show your concern and get clarification.)

Use Explorer Groups

Explorer groups go to other businesses to see how they do things. When you hear about a great idea another business is using, send out an explorer group to scope it out. One supermarket known for exceptional service encourages employees to take a company van and rush to the scene of good service given by others. They take notes and discuss possible implementation in their store. Explorer groups need not be sent only to direct competitors; often businesses have great ideas you can use.

Another way to gather great data is to "explore" how your own organization is serving customers by being a customer. Call the company and note the impression created by the person answering the phone. Is this what your customer is hearing? How do you like it? Then visit other locations or areas in your own organization and see how you are treated.

Call your own company and see how you are treated.

Try "Mystery Shopping"

Use "mystery shoppers" to visit company locations posing as customers. Trained shoppers—usually provided by outside shopper services—look for specific behaviors or processes and report their results back to management and the employees who served them. For example, a friend of mine owned several barber shops. He developed a checklist of things he wanted each of his hair stylists to do, twelve in all. They included such things as promptly greeting customers with a smile, introducing themselves by name, asking how customers like their hair cut, looking directly at customers as they answer, calling customers by name, maintaining a clean work area, etc. He then recruited shoppers, and gave them the money for the haircut and a checklist. Immediately after having their hair cut, the shoppers left the shop, filled out the check sheet, and then returned to the shop to reward the stylist by giving a dollar tip for each item checked. The system gave immediate feedback and reinforced what management wanted its employees to do.

Mystery shopping is best when it is systematically done and the results are used to reinforce positive employee behaviors rather than to catch them doing things wrong. Be certain to have a specific checklist so that each employee "shopped" is measured with the same yardstick.

> Mystery shopping works best when it is used to reward employees, not to catch them doing things wrong.

The activity at the end of this chapter teaches you how to be a mystery shopper.

Use Focus Groups

Focus groups have long been used for marketing research, but they can also play an important role in understanding customer perceptions and expectations.

Although some marketing consultants may disagree with me, there's no great mystery to how focus groups work, and any intelligent person can run one effectively. Here is the procedure:

- Select a random sample of your customers or patrons to participate in the focus group session. Don't pick just people you know or customers you like. You may, however, want to be sure they are among your better customers by qualifying them according to their influence or how much they spend with you. You can get customer names off their checks, credit cards, or other records.
- Formally invite the customers to participate, telling them when and where as well as how long the session will take. Let them know the reason: that you are attempting to better understand customer needs and ways you can better be of service to them.

- Keep your focus group to about a dozen people. Ask customers to confirm their attendance but expect that some will not show up. Fifteen confirmed reservations generally get you 12 actual participants. Follow up with phone calls to confirm attendance. (One supermarket I worked with was so excited about the focus groups that they invited 40 or 50 people every month! The problem, of course, is that a group that large makes it hard for all people to be heard. Some people dominated the group while others, who had equally good ideas but were uncomfortable speaking before so many people, suppressed their ideas.)
- Reward focus group participants. Compensate people with merchandise, a gift certificate, a free dinner, or cash. In marketing research, it's not uncommon to pay people $50 or more for a one- or two-hour session.

> Keep focus groups diverse, to about a dozen people, and comfortable.

TO GET THE MOST FROM FOCUS GROUPS:

- Set the stage by having either an independent consultant or someone from top management moderate the group.
- Create an open atmosphere where participants feel comfortable giving all kinds of feedback. Be polite, open, encouraging, and receptive.
- Avoid cutting people off when they're making a critical comment. Do not, above all, be defensive of the way you're doing things now, when in the eyes of the customer it's not working.
- Keep any follow-up questions open-ended. Don't interrogate.
- As focus group members express compliments, acknowledge them and express thanks. Then make a statement such as, "We're happy to hear that we are doing things you like, but our major purpose here is to identify ways that we can do a better job in meeting your needs. How can we do even better?"
- Limit the group to a predetermined amount of time; typically a one-hour or (maximum) 90-minute session works best. Any longer than that and you start losing people's interest.
- Tape record the entire focus group session and transcribe key notes for review. As you analyze the results of this group session, look for key words that might tip you off to what the customers are looking for. If, for example, concerns about the amount of time needed to complete their transactions come up repeatedly, you might make a mental note of how you might meet customer needs more quickly.
- At the end of the focus group session, be sure to thank the participants for all of their input—and give them their pay.

Try Customer Feedback Cards

Many organizations solicit feedback via printed cards that customers can fill out and send back to management. While such cards can provide an outlet for customers and occasionally generate some useful data, feedback cards have several drawbacks:

> Feedback card systems have drawbacks.

- Only people who are very satisfied or very dissatisfied complete the cards. You get the comments on both extremes but less data from the middle—those customers who are somewhat neutral.
- Some cards ask the wrong questions. Designing the card calls for research skills to be sure you are getting valid data. I recall a restaurant feedback card that had a long list of yes–no response questions about food portion size, temperature, price, etc. I wanted to comment about the server but found nowhere on the card to do so.
- Occasionally cards require too much of the customer. While questionnaire formats can be limiting, open-ended cards may ask too much of customers' ability to express themselves. Believe it or not, I've also seen cards that require the customer to provide the postage.
- Sometimes the card fails to tell the customer what to do with it. Some can be submitted only in a drop box in the store or restaurant.

Overall, feedback cards are less useful than the other methods of finding out about customer concerns. The apparent ease of having a feedback card system makes it attractive for companies too lazy to go after better data.

Service Snapshot

Monika's Attitude of Service

Monika works at a medium-sized credit union. In her two years there she has won repeated awards and bonuses for her effectiveness as a teller and member services representative. Her supervisor consistently ranks Monika's work as outstanding, and her opportunities in the financial service industry look rosy. When I asked her about her customer service "technique," she laughed and said she doesn't really have a techniques, she just tries to treat people the way she'd want to be treated.

Monika pays attention to the little things, avoiding the people turnoffs as much as possible. When a member approaches her desk, she immediately looks up and says hello with a smile. If she's busy helping someone else, she at least makes eye contact to acknowledge the customer and let the member know she'll be there in a moment. She is especially good at handling transactions quickly and efficiently without rushing the customer. When I asked her how she prepared for her career, she told me that when she was a little girl her favorite toy was a cash register. She loved to play store and keep Monopoly money in a special section in the cash drawer. She even used to iron her play money to keep it crisp, she said laughingly!

Technique aside, Monika projects a friendly, helpful attitude. She works hard to keep current on changes in systems and procedures and gives her employer 110 percent effort every day. She loves her job. Serving others with professionalism and skill is its own reward, she says.

Another Look

They Complain Because They Care[9]

Successfully resolving customer complaints can boost profits by increasing loyalty.

"When complaints are heard freely, deeply considered, and speedily reformed, then is the utmost bound of civil liberty attained that wise men look for." John Milton said that in 1644. More than 300 years later, smart retailers pay heed to his words. In many ways, complaining customers are the best kind of business.

"It seems kind of funny, thinking about the complainer as someone who cares," says Amanda Purs, director of research and development for Cincinnati-based Burke Customer Satisfaction Associates. "But we found that if you're satisfied with a store, you're more likely to complain when something goes wrong." Complainers are likely to feel loyal to stores that trigger their outbursts, according to a Burke telephone survey of 1,179 randomly selected department store shoppers. Furthermore, grousers are likely to remain loyal even after the incidents that displease them.

If this sounds similar to the tried-and-true parental motto, "I yell because I care," it's because the concept is the same. Parents yell because they have an enormous stake in raising their children. Shoppers often take the time to complain because they feel connected to a particular store. Rather than dumping it for another, they'll expend energy to try to make it perform the way they think it should.

Burke unearthed insights about complaining customers as a byproduct of an attempt to learn more about "secure customers"—those who feel great satisfaction with a store, would recommend it to others, and would shop there again. As it turns out, secure customers and complainers have similar profiles. Secure customers tend to be women aged 45 and older who shop at department stores at least once a month. Complainers are split evenly between men and women, but they are also likely to be older, frequent shoppers. In contrast, the most "vulnerable" customers are infrequent shoppers under age 35.

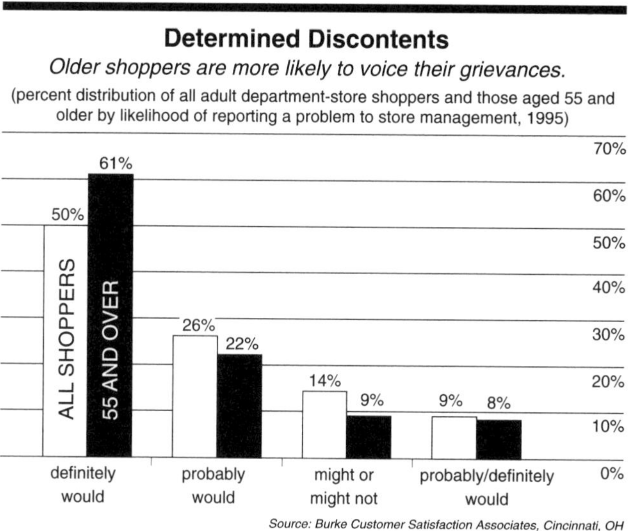

Half of respondents say they definitely would report a problem to store management, and the likelihood of doing so increases greatly with age. Sixty-one percent of the 55-and-older set would complain, compared with 39 percent of those under age 35. Older people are also more likely to expect results, which may be part of the reason why they are willing to make the effort in the first place. Nearly half of older complainers but just one in five younger complainers expect stores to resolve problems satisfactorily.

Many of the people who say they would complain might not carry through, says Prus. Some don't want to spend the time, and others feel the time will be wasted. This makes the actual complaining customer a rare and special person indeed. JC Penney tries hard to accommodate and learn from such customers. In any of its 1,250 stores, "only the store manager has the final authority to say 'no'" to a customer's request for satisfaction, says corporate spokesman Hank Rusman.

Penney's also has discovered that its efforts in patching up disagreements go a long way toward strengthening customer loyalty. The Burke study confirms this notion. Shoppers who encounter problems and get stores to resolve them feel even better about the store than if things always go smoothly. "It's as if you were served a lousy meal at a restaurant, and the chef cooked you a whole new meal. That's what you'd remember and talk about," says Prus.

Cooking that extra meal is time-consuming, but worthwhile. Retailers and service providers of all shapes and sizes should think hard about how to handle malcontents, because they may see more of them in the future. Customer expectations are on the rise, and today's shoppers compare the treatment they receive not only from department store to department store, but from dentist to drug store to dry cleaner.

Burke Customer Satisfaction Associates incorporates the Secure Customer Index into most research for its clients; contact Amanda Prus at (513) 684-7607. For tips on how to turn complaints to advantage, see "The Sales Behind the Scowl" in the March/April 1996 issue of our sister publication, *Marketing Tools;* telephone (800) 828-1133.

—Tibbett L. Speer

A FINAL THOUGHT

Moving customers from the zone of indifference where they may be reasonably satisfied into the category of motivated, loyal fans requires close and repeated checks of the ways we may be turning them off. This needs to be an ongoing process, not just an occasional set of actions. If we have made mistakes that leave customers unhappy, we need to view this as an opportunity for solidifying a relationship with good recovery skills. We also need to continually seek information to direct the kinds of changes that reduce the number of value, systems, and people turnoffs. This is the first step to earning customer loyalty. The second step, exceeding customer expectations, is the topic of Chapter 4. But first, in Chapter 3, we'll look in more depth at ways to deal with the dissatisfied customer.

Summary of Key Ideas

- All people have pet peeves about how they are served (or not served). These are often little things that have a cumulative effect in creating dissatisfaction or, minimally, an indifferent customer.
- The impact of many little things can have a dramatic effect on an organization's or an individual's success. These little things can work to our advantage or disadvantage.
- Customer turnoffs can be usefully categorized into value, systems, and people problems. Value and system problems are best addressed by company leaders; everyone can help eliminate people problems, primarily through improving interpersonal skills.
- People turnoffs are almost always communication problems. Employees communicate inappropriate "messages" by their words or nonverbal actions.
- Value is a function of a product's apparent quality relative to its cost.

- The term *systems* refers to anything involved with getting the product or service to the customer. It involves a wide range of procedures, policies, and systematic actions.
- Service recovery involves winning back customers when they have had a disappointing experience. Customers whose problems are addressed by the company will actually be more likely to do business there again than will the customer who never had a problem.
- Customer loyalty emerges when service *is* your business, not just an added dynamic. The term "service department" is redundant. All departments are in the service business first.
- We can best reduce customer turnoffs by actively listening to customer concerns, using explorer groups to see what others are doing, using mystery shoppers to test our own service, conducting periodic focus groups to better understand what customers want or need, and gathering feedback card data.
- Although feedback cards are widely used, they often present drawbacks that contaminate the data received. These problems can be overcome with other data-gathering approaches.

Key Terms and Concepts

Active listening
Customer loyalty
Explorer groups
Feedback cards
Focus groups
Mystery shoppers
People turnoffs
System turnoffs
Systematic observation
The "zone of indifference"
Value turnoffs

Self-Test Questions

1. What kinds of little things make a difference in customer service? Give examples of some little things companies use to set themselves apart from competitors.
2. How do a customer's expectations affect customer service?
3. What are the three categories of customer turnoffs? Give an example of each.
4. How important is it to get customers out of the "zone of indifference"? What are the two important steps necessary to accomplish this?
5. How can listening skills be used to improve customer satisfaction?
6. What is an explorer group, and how can it be used to boost a company's customer service?
7. What kinds of things can a "mystery shopper" find out about a business' customer service?
8. What are the steps to running a successful focus group?
9. Explain the pros and cons of using customer feedback cards.

Application Activity: Let's Go Mystery Shopping

Select a minimum of four businesses of the same type (retailers, restaurants, banks, car dealers, whatever) to visit as a mystery shopper. Your task is to pose as a potential shopper seeking information. You may want information about account types from a bank, details on a computer or appliance from electronics stores, information about an automobile, etc.

Be yourself during these visits. Don't attempt to act. Respond naturally to the employees. Don't go in with the attitude that you'll catch them doing something wrong.

Immediately after each visit, complete an evaluation form. You may design your own form or use one like the sample included here.

Sample Mystery Shopper Form[10]

Name of business:________________ Date & time:____________

Employee's name ________________ Task: ________________
(if available) (*what you are shopping for*)

	Did	*Did Not*
A. When you entered, did the employee:		
1. Look up, make eye contact?	____	____
2. Smile with a genuine smile?	____	____
3. Acknowledge you with an appropriate greeting?	____	____
4. Make you wait too long before helping you?	____	____
B. While assisting you, did the employee:		
5. Project a positive, helpful attitude and willingness to assist?	____	____
6. Pay full and undivided attention to you?	____	____
7. Deliver accurate, speedy, but unhurried service?	____	____
8. Ask you if there was anything else he/she can do for you?	____	____
C. Given the opportunity to offer or introduce other products, did the employee:		
9. Acknowledge or identify other things that may meet your needs?	____	____
10. Offer further information or introduce you to others for more information?	____	____
11. Ask you for your business?	____	____
D. When the transaction was over, did the employee:		
12. Thank you for coming in?	____	____
13. Invite you to come again?	____	____
14. Offer a friendly goodbye?	____	____
E. At any time during the transaction, did the employee:		
15. Ask for your name and/or call you by name?	____	____
16. Make you feel like a valued customer?	____	____
Score one point for each "Did" answer. Total	____	____

General comments or observations: What was particularly good or bad about the shopping experience? ____________________

____

____

____

____

____

____

Ground rules: Don't go in with a chip on your shoulder and don't overemphasize the negative. If you can't remember whether the employee did or did not do something positive, assume that he or she did.

When you have gathered your data from four or more locations, compile a brief report on what you found. If you owned this business, what would you do to improve the service? Be specific.

NOTES

[1]T. Peters, "Service or Perish," *Forbes ASAP,* December 4, 1995, p. 142.

[2]This story is covered in detail in "From Beetle to Bedraggled: Behind VW's Stunning U.S. Decline," *Advertising Age,* September 13, 1993.

[3]Excerpted from R. McGarvey, "Little Things Do Mean a Lot," *Reader's Digest,* June 1993, p. 33.

[4]K. DeTienne and P. Timm, "How Well Do Businesses Predict Customer Turnoffs?: A Discrepancy Analysis," *Journal of Marketing Management,* 1996.

[5]Excerpted from an advertising piece by Nightingale-Conant Corporation advertising, M. Gerber's "The E-Myth Seminar" audiotape program. Nightingale-Conant, 1996. This tape program can be purchased from N-C at 1-800-525-9000.

[6]F. Herzberg, B. Mausner, and B. Snyderman, *The Motivation to Work,* 2nd ed. (New York: Wiley, 1959).

[7]B. Sanders, *Fabled Service* (San Diego: Pfeiffer & Company, 1995), p. 9.

[8]Sanders, p. 3.

[9]T. L. Speer, "They Complain Because They Care" is reprinted from *American Demographics,* May 1996, pp. 13–14. Reprinted with permission of Dow-Jones Publishing and *American Demographics.*

[10]This mystery shopper form was developed by the author and is copyrighted. Permission is granted to use this for educational purposes; however, any commercial use requires written approval from the author. Call Dr. Paul R. Timm at 801.356.7102; fax: 707.276.1048; or e-mail DrTimm@aol.com.

Foundation Skill 3

Deal with Dissatisfied Customers

Here's an Opportunity for You

Those who enter to buy, support me. Those who come to flatter, please me. Those who complain, teach me how I may please others so that more will come. Those only hurt me who are displeased but do not complain. They refuse me permission to correct my errors and thus improve my service.

—Retailing pioneer Marshall Field

WHAT YOU'LL LEARN IN THIS CHAPTER

- Customer retention requires positive attitudes toward problem solving. This does not necessarily mean that the customer is always right.
- Who is right or who is wrong is not the key issue in customer disputes. All parties can cooperate to solve the customer's concerns.
- A customer complaint is an opportunity to cement a relationship and create customer loyalty.
- Recovery skills are necessary to career success and will be regularly used.

- The key skills in recovery involve feeling the customer's "pain," doing all you can to resolve the problem, and then going the extra step via "symbolic atonement."
- Chronic complainers can best be handled by understanding their motives and then getting them to propose an acceptable solution.
- Effective written communication uses human relations principles such as reader self-interest, reader-centeredness, and individual treatment to best deal with customer concerns.
- Abrasiveness is a drawback to customer relations, while assertiveness leads to better problem resolution.

The Way It Is

Customer Complaints May Lead to Repeat Business

Successful handling of customer complaints can be a gold mine of repeat business. Statistics from surveys reported by the U.S. Office of Consumer Affairs reveal some interesting facts. Among these:

1. One customer in four is dissatisfied with some aspect of a typical transaction.
2. A dissatisfied customer, on average, will complain to 12 other people about the company that provided poor service.
3. Only 5 percent of dissatisfied customers complain to the company. The vast "silent majority" would rather switch than fight. They take their business elsewhere.

But there is good news for companies that learn to effectively handle complaints. Such companies can charge an average of 8 percent to 15 percent more than their competitors, even in businesses where competition is keen. (Example: Maytag, the quality home appliance maker with the "lonely repairman" campaign, supports a premium-priced product in a highly price-sensitive market.)

The best news of all is that customers who have their complaints handled well are very likely to do business with the company again. While only 9 to 37 percent of dissatisfied customers who don't complain report a willingness to do business with the same company again, fully 50 percent to 80 percent of those whose complaints are fully resolved will consider doing repeat business—even if their complaints were not resolved in their favor![1]

Customer recovery isn't always easy, but it is tremendously profitable.

We talked in Chapter 2 about the importance of reducing the turnoffs. These efforts are worthwhile, but reality tells us that we cannot predict with certainty every possible customer complaint. In short, dissatisfaction happens. What we choose to do about it can go a long way toward creating customer loyalty. It's not always easy, but saving customers can be enormously profitable. Effective complaint handling begins with the right attitudes coupled with the skills we'll discuss in this chapter.

MAINTAIN A HEALTHY CUSTOMER RETENTION ATTITUDE

The discussion in Chapter 1 about the value of customers should be firmly implanted in your mind. The best attitudes for service providers stem from the desire for a win–win relationship with the customer. Both parties want to feel good about the business transacted. This is not necessarily a "customer is always right" attitude. Restaurant owner Jeffery Mount explains:

> When I bought my restaurant, in 1981, I wanted it to become cutting edge: customer-centered, employee empowered, socially responsible. I read the business rags and listened to the gurus for the newest and the greatest teachings. Everywhere I went I heard businesspeople chant the mantra that the customer is always right.
>
> I even proudly hung on my wall that ubiquitous sign, which is plastered on walls of progressive companies throughout the land: *Rule #1: The customer is always right. Rule #2: If the customer is wrong, see rule #1.* I all but insisted that my staff pledge their allegiance to the infallible customer.
>
> My, how times have changed. There's no way you'll hear me say now that the customer is always right. We wouldn't be doing ourselves or our customers a favor by insisting on that.[2]

We'll come back to some examples from Mount's restaurant in a moment, but why do you think he changed his ideas about the customer being right? The answer lies in the fact that customers, just like you or me, at times make mistakes or demand unreasonable things. The oversimplified attitude about the customer's "rightness" is far less productive than one that says, "I will do my best to provide the customer with satisfaction (and more) whether the customer is right or wrong. What matters is an attitude of wanting to solve the problem at hand."

> The "rightness" or "wrongness" of a customer isn't the issue. What matters is wanting to solve customer problems.

Jeffery Mount illustrates with a story about a customer who is clearly wrong but who was treated in a manner that solves the problem and builds loyalty:

> Recently, a customer ordered finger sandwiches for a business luncheon. We advised against it. Wrong product, we warned her; too dainty, too small to

> feed hungry men and women at midday. Serve our hearty deli sandwiches, we suggested. "Oh, no," she replied. She insisted on finger sandwiches. Guess who called up, panicking, because "these sandwiches aren't going to be enough food"? "No problem," we said. We quickly created a bodacious big sandwich platter and delivered it in a New York minute. Even made a little money along the way.[3]

The issue was *not* whether the customer or the company was right. The attitude was one of cooperation and problem solving that won Mount's restaurant a loyal customer.

In addition to a problem-solving rather than blame-setting attitude, service recovery is best handled as an opportunity rather than as a painful chore. Granted, most of us would prefer not to hear about customers' dissatisfaction. That's human nature. But given that dissatisfaction does occur, an attitude of accepting the opportunity and challenge can be useful. Customer complaints are opportunities to cement relationships. The vast majority of such relationships are worth saving, although occasionally—I stress *occasionally*—we need to let go of the chronic complainer, as we'll discuss later in this chapter.

> Complaints are opportunities to cement relationships and create customer loyalty.

Self-Analysis

What Are Your Feelings about Dealing with Difficult Customers?

The following list of words may describe how you feel about dealing with upset customers. Select the five that most describe your general feelings. When you have finished this chapter, review these words to see if you have some better ideas on how to deal with these emotions. Discuss your results in a small group, asking for their feedback on how to deal with your feelings.

afraid	cautious	eager	glad	relieved
angry	comfortable	ecstatic	hesitant	sad
anxious	confident	elated	humiliated	silly
apathetic	confused	excited	joyful	uncomfortable
bored	contented	foolish	nervous	uneasy
calm	distraught	frustrated	proud	wishful

My Top Five

1. ______________________
2. ______________________
3. ______________________
4. ______________________
5. ______________________

DEVELOP YOUR RECOVERY SKILLS

Customer service is easy when nothing goes wrong. However, a study by the Technical Assistance Research Program (TARP) estimates that approximately one in every four purchases results in some form of customer problem experience.[4]

Employees often underestimate the negative ripple effects caused by even one unhappy customer. To reduce the impact of such ripples, we need to develop *recovery skills.* As the name implies, we try to recover the potentially lost customer. We can best do this by remembering three steps:

1. Feel Their Pain

The first step in recovery is to recognize that upset customers are likely to be disappointed, angry, frustrated, or even in pain, and they blame you to some extent. Typically they want you to do some or all of the following:

- Listen to their concerns and take them seriously.
- Understand their problem and the reason they are upset.
- Compensate them or provide restitution for the unsatisfactory product or service.
- Share their sense of urgency, get their problem handled quickly.
- Prevent further inconvenience.
- Treat them with respect and empathy.
- Have someone punished for the problem (sometimes).
- Assure them the problem will not happen again.

You may not need to do all these things in every situation, but typically the upset customer requires several of them.

2. Do All You Can to Resolve the Problem

When attempting to recover an unhappy customer, look for ways to fix the situation and give something extra to make up for the problem. Jeffery Mount's restaurant recovered the customer who ordered too little food by rushing in with the "bodacious sandwich platter." No matter that they tried to dissuade the customer from ordering the wrong food in the first place. They fixed it with something extra—a quick rescue.

Suppose you buy a new pair of shoes and the heel falls off. You call the shoe store and the owner says to bring them back and he'll replace them. You take time off work, drive downtown to the store, battle for a parking space, and spend about an hour doing this. He cheerfully gives you a new pair of shoes. Are you satisfied now?

Probably not. Why? Because he really hasn't repaid you for your inconvenience. Sure, he stood behind the product and perhaps even did so in a pleasant manner, but you still came out on the short end. Fixing the problem is good, but probably not enough.

3. Go Beyond: Offer "Symbolic Atonement"

What kinds of things can we do to reconcile for the problem? Much of the remainder of this book deals with this topic. Meanwhile, here are a few ideas that could be seen as going the extra mile in the eyes of a customer:

- *Offer to pick up or deliver* goods to be replaced or repaired. Lexus got a lot of mileage out of offering to pick up recalled cars rather than having customers bring them in.
- *Give a gift* of merchandise to repay for the inconvenience. The gift may be small but the thought will be appreciated. Customer service expert Ron Zemke calls this "symbolic atonement." Things like a free dessert for the restaurant customer who endures slow service or extra copies of a print job to offset a minor delay are examples. It's the thought that counts.
- *Reimburse* for costs of returning merchandise such as parking fees, etc. (Mail order retailers pay all return postage fees to reduce customer annoyance and inconvenience.)
- *Acknowledge* customers' inconvenience and thank them for giving you the opportunity to try to make it right. A sincere apology can go a long way. Make the wording of the apology sincere and personal. Say, "I'm sorry you had to wait," rather than, "The company regrets the delay." Empathy can be expressed with statements like, "I know how aggravating it can be to . . ." or "I hate when that happens and I'm sorry you had to go through . . ."
- *Follow up to see that the problem was handled.* Don't assume the customer's difficulty has been fixed unless you handled it yourself and have checked with the customer to see that the fix held up.

You may not have the authority to do all these things (although many of these cost practically nothing), but you can go to bat for the customer with your boss. Just being the customer's advocate can help reduce much of the problem. If all goes well, you should feel a genuine sense of satisfaction after handling an unhappy or irate customer.

> If you don't have the authority to do what's needed to save the customer, become an advocate. Go to bat for the customer with your boss.

What Happens If the Customer Is Still Not Satisfied?

Often you can creatively recover an unhappy customer, but this is not a perfect world and people are not always rational; so sometimes you too get upset. Professionalism requires that you do everything possible to avoid letting your anger or frustration show through to the customer or other customers.

The key things to remember are:

- If you *try your best to satisfy* the customer, you have done all that you can do.
- *Don't take it personally.* Upset people often say things they don't really mean. They are blowing off steam, venting frustration. If the problem was really your fault, resolve to learn from the experience and do better next time. If you had no control over the situation, do what you can, but don't bat your head against the wall.
- *Don't rehash the experience* with your coworkers or in your own mind. What's done is done. Recounting the experience with others probably won't make their day any better and rehashing it to yourself will just make you mad. You may, however, want to ask another person how he or she would have handled the situation.
- Use every customer contact experience as an *opportunity to improve* your professionalism. Even the most unpleasant encounter can teach us useful lessons.

LOOK BACK AND LEARN FROM EACH SITUATION

When the customer situation has cooled, you may want to review it with an eye toward improving your skills. Think where you used your recovery skills and ask questions like these:

- What was the nature of the customer's complaint? Was it primarily value-, systems-, or people-generated?
- How did the customer see the problem? Who was to blame? What irritated the customer most? Why was he or she angry or frustrated?
- How did you see the problem? Was the customer partially to blame?
- What did you say to the customer that helped the situation?
- What did you say that seemed to aggravate the situation?
- How did you show your concern to the customer?
- What would you do differently?
- Do you think this customer will do business with you again? Why or why not?

Make careful notes of your responses to these questions to build your confidence and professionalism.

> Review how you handled a situation with an eye toward improving your skills and professionalism.

HANDLE THE OCCASIONAL CUSTOMER FROM HELL

"Stubbornness is the energy of fools," says the German proverb. Sometimes we need to draw the line between upset customers with legitimate problems and chronic complainers who consume our time with unreasonable demands—the dreaded "customer from hell."

Be Sure This Really Is a Chronic Complainer

Step one in dealing with such people is to be sure you've got a chronic complainer. When you've tried the normal recovery approaches and nothing seems to work, look for the following telltale signs:[5]

Occasionally we meet a chronic complainer.

- They always look for someone to blame. In their world accidents don't happen: Someone is always at fault, and it's probably you.
- They never admit any degree of fault or responsibility. They see themselves as blameless and victims of the incompetence or malice of others.
- They have strong ideas about what others should do. They love to define other peoples' duties. If you hear a complaint phrased exclusively in terms of what other people always, never, must, or must not do, chances are you're talking to a chronic complainer.

- They complain at length. While normal complainers pause for breath every now and then, chronics seem able to inhale while saying the words, "and another thing . . . ."

What to Do with This Guy (or Gal)

When faced with that occasional chronic complainer (they really are quite rare, fortunately), try these techniques:

- Actively listen to identify the legitimate grievance beneath the endless griping. Rephrase the complainer's main points in your own words, even if you have to interrupt to do so. Say something like, "Excuse me, but do I understand you to say that the package didn't arrive on time and you feel frustrated and annoyed?"
- Establish the facts to reduce the complainer's tendency to exaggerate or overgeneralize. If he says he "tried calling all day but as usual you tried to avoid me," establish the actual number of times called and when.
- Resist the temptation to apologize, although that may seem to be the natural thing to do. Since the main thing the complainer is trying to do is fix blame—not solve problems—your apology will be seen as an open invitation to further blaming. Instead, ask questions like, "Would an extended warranty solve your problem?" or "When would be the best time for me to call you back with that information?"
- Force the complainer to pose solutions to the problem, especially if she doesn't seem to like your ideas. Also, try putting a time limit on the conversation by saying something like, "I have to talk with someone in 10 minutes. What sort of action plan can we work out in that time?" The object of this is to get her away from whining and into a problem-solving mode.

We have, of course, no guarantees when dealing with such customers, but the effort may well be worth it. Converting one of these folks into a normal, rational customer can be professionally rewarding. If it doesn't work, so be it. You've given your best and that's all anyone can ask.

> Get the chronic complainer to pose possible solutions to the problem rather than just dwell on blaming someone.

A Prentice-Hall booklet called *The Customer Service Manager's Handbook of People Power Strategies* includes a section called "10 'Buzz Phrases' That Help You Disarm Irate Customers." Commit these to memory, use them frequently until they become comfortable and just roll off your tongue, and see how they can dramatically enhance your success with people in conflict situations.

Some Useful "Buzz Phrases" When Dealing with Upset Customers:[6]

1. **"Anyone in your position . . ."** The suggestion here is that the customer holds an important job or social rank. Don't be afraid to lard it on. No one ever gets tired of being told how good they look or how important they are.
2. **"I'd sure appreciate it if . . ."** This phrase implicitly asks the customer's permission, suggesting that the customer has the power to grant or refuse.
3. **"You could really help me by . . ."** Suggests that the customer is not only taking a hand in the complaint-resolution process, but is also taking something of a parental or "older brother" role.
4. **Perhaps you could give me some advice . . ."** Makes the customer into a veritable fount of wisdom.
5. **"Because of your specialized knowledge . . ."** Suggests a high degree of skill or advanced study. People love to think that others view them as highly intelligent.
6. **"Someone of your attainments . . ."** Suggests that the customer is a great success in life.
7. **"As you, of course, know . . ."** Suggests vast learning. This phrase is especially effective when you are telling customers something you know that they don't know. Most people don't like to admit that they are ignorant, even of things that they have no reason to know.
8. **"You're absolutely right about that . . ."** A routine but effective "stroke." Use it to readily concede some minor point the customer makes. The customer will then be more willing to give ground on the major points of contention.
9. **"Someone as busy as you are . . ."** Implies that the customer is one of the world's movers and shakers. Also implies that the problem will be resolved as quickly as possible.
10. **"I'd sure be grateful if . . ."** Suggests an easy way to make someone happy, a natural human drive.

Note that some of these phrases start with "I," a word you should normally avoid in confrontations with customers. You can use it safely here because you are using "I" in a totally nonchallenging way. If you are feeling more aggressive, however, and a more confrontational approach seems in order, just start your remarks with the word "you."

HANDLE A NASTY COMPLAINT LETTER

Today's customers don't write very often but when they do, it reflects a significant effort. Perhaps because they are fairly rare, letters carry considerable impact. Letters provide a graphic and tangible reminder of a customer's dissatisfaction and have a nasty habit of appearing in your personnel file. So it makes sense to respond to them and to document what you've done.

If you choose to respond to a letter with a phone call, be certain to have the letter in front of you and to refer to the specific points as written. Also, make notes of what the customer says and how you respond. If you respond to a letter with a letter of your own, be certain that your letter conveys a problem-solving attitude, projects goodwill, and conveys professionalism.

Be an effective writer by applying the same human relations skills you would use in a face-to-face encounter. Specifically, be sensitive to people's feelings, interests, wants, and needs. Failure to do so creates unnecessary strains on relationships. Since a letter is a hard copy of a conversation, it is especially important that it be tactful. A poorly written document will come back to haunt you.

> Apply human relations skills to your writing. A poorly written letter will come back to haunt you.

USE THE 3 F'S—FEEL, FELT, FOUND[7]—TO DISARM THE UPSET CUSTOMER

Seminar leader and author Rebecca Morgan teaches people how to express ideas so that upset customers won't become more upset. She describes the "3 F's" technique:

The 3 F's are a skeleton on which to hang the rest of your response to a customer. This technique acknowledges customers' feelings and offers an explanation in a way they can listen to. For example, "I understand how you could *feel* that way. Others have *felt* that way too. And then they *found,* after an explanation, that this policy actually protects them, so it made sense."

Try using the 3 F's approach as Morgan does. Be careful how you word it. Do not say, "I know how you feel" (you really can't know exactly how another person feels) but do say, "I can understand how (or why) you'd feel that way."

USE HUMAN RELATIONS SKILLS TO CONVEY APPROPRIATE TONE

Let's consider a few principles of human relations[8] and how these might apply in communication with unhappy customers. The first and perhaps most basic principle is that . . .

1. People Are Strongly Interested in Themselves

It is the nature of the human being—and all other known creatures, for that matter—to be concerned with and motivated by their own personal needs, wants, and interests. This self-centeredness, or egocentricity, is normal and not particularly harmful unless carried to the extreme, when there is *no* caring about others.

> Our primary motivation is self-interest.

When people speak or write, they reflect this egocentricity in their language. A study conducted at a Midwestern university showed that every fifth word written or spoken by a human being is *I* or one of its derivations—*me, mine, my, we, ours, us.*[9]

Even though we are all self-centered to some degree, most of us learn to temper the tendency to focus on and talk about ourselves exclusively. Indeed, the extremely egocentric person is avoided like someone with a contagious disease.

> You can turn a person's natural egocentricity into an advantage by recognizing his or her needs.

The point is that business writers can turn this egocentricity into an advantage if they recognize the reader's needs. Effective communicators learn to express concern and appreciation for the views of others in letters, memos, reports, proposals, and other documents.

2. People Prefer Receiver-Centered Messages

One important way to reflect consideration for another person is to phrase your message in terms of their viewpoint. Expressing appropriate viewpoint involves much more than just selecting certain key words. Genuine receiver viewpoint causes a document's tone to reflect a sincere interest in the other person. Self-centered writers and talkers think of themselves first. Receiver-oriented writ-

> The receiver-oriented communicator thinks of the other person first.

ers think of and convey their messages in terms of what the message receiver wants or needs.

One "red flag" that we should look for are the words *I, me, my,* and so forth found in abundance in our messages. Second or third person (*you*, or the impersonal, *one*) often conveys more receiver interest and objectivity.

Please don't conclude that you should try to *eliminate* the use of *I* and its variations. To do so may be impossible in some cases. In other cases, your efforts may result in rather tortured syntax and excessive wordiness. Besides, the use of *I, we,* or *me* does not always indicate a lack of reader viewpoint. For example, if you say, "I hope you will be happy with this decision," you are not really violating a receiver viewpoint even though the sentence begins with the word *I*. The overall tone and sense of caring for the other person are far more important than simply avoiding the use of first-person pronouns.

Look at the following sample sentences and see the difference in the tone of the receiver-oriented version compared to the "*I*-centered" one:

***I*-CENTERED**	**RECEIVER VIEWPOINT**
We require that you sign the sales slip before we charge this purchase to your account.	For your protection, we charge your account only after you have signed the sales slip.
I have been a sales professional for 22 years.	My 22 years' experience as a sales professional provides a strong background in understanding customer concerns.
I am sending your software back to you for an update.	So that you may update this software to the most current version, it is being returned to you.
I'd like to show you this life insurance plan.	As a young father, you'll be interested in a life insurance plan tailored to the couple with small children and a limited budget.

Phrasing ideas in terms of the receiver's viewpoint conveys an interest in the other person and recognizes a principle of good human relations.

3. People Want to Be Treated As Individuals

We can improve the tone of written documents by phrasing our information as though talking to individuals, rather than groups. A personally addressed business letter singles out a reader for individual attention.

> The sweetest sound to most people is the sound of their own names.

Such a letter conveys a more sincere regard for the specific person than one addressed to "Dear Customer" or "Dear Fellow Employee."

Names or other information can be easily inserted while most of the letter remains the same for all readers. Explore these possibilities when you consider developing form letters to deal with recurrent situations.

Avoid the "Blanket Tone"

When a document makes the reader feel lost in the crowd, the "blanket tone" is responsible. For example, consider the blanket tone in the following excerpts:

> The blanket tone makes the reader feel lost in the crowd.

BLANKET TONE	MORE PERSONAL TONE
When a thousand requests are received from prospective customers, we feel pleased. These requests show that our product is well received.	A copy of the booklet you requested is being sent to you today. Thank you for requesting it.
The cooperation of our charge customers in paying their accounts is appreciated. By paying on time, they allow us to give better service.	I certainly appreciate your paying the account. Your prompt payment allows us to give you better service and keep prices down.

4. Address Your Receiver Directly

Strive to express ideas in terms of the individual's benefit. One way to do this is through direct address—statements that say, "This means you!" Each day we see examples of this approach in television and radio commercials. The announcer "personally" addresses each of the several million people who may be listening and attempts to make them feel that they are spoken to as individuals. Direct address shows your receivers how your message applies to them and how it can meet their individual needs in some way.

5. Give People Positive Information

Positive language often conveys more information than negative language. It also tends to be more upbeat with a more pleasant tone. Rather than telling a person what is *not* possible or what you *cannot* do, focus on the positive—what is possible or what you *can* do. If you say "I *cannot* give cash refunds on sale merchandise," you convey only negative information. It does not say what you can do; it only rules out one of the possibilities. On the other hand, if you say, "I can arrange to have the product exchanged for another model that may better meet your needs," the statement conveys specific and positive information.

Positive language also has a pleasant ring to the ear. Yet many common negative phrases still creep into business writing. For example:

> We *regret* to inform you that we cannot . . .
>
> We have received your *claim* . . . [Claim has a negative ring for most people.]
>
> Your *failure* to comply . . .

Here is an example to illustrate the difference in tone between positive and negative word choices. A corporate executive wrote to a local civic group denying a request to use the company's meeting facilities. To soften the refusal, however, the executive decided to let the group use a conference room, which might be somewhat small for its purpose, but was probably better than no room at all. Unfortunately, the executive was not sensitive to the effects of negative wording. She wrote:

> We regret to inform you that we cannot permit you to use our company training room for your meeting, because the Beardstown Ladies' Investment Club asked for it first. This group has a standing date to use our place the third Thursday of every month. We can, however, let you use our conference room; but it seats only 25.

Review of the word connotations clearly brings out the negative words (*regret, cannot, seats only 25*) first, while the otherwise positive message (*you can use the conference room*) is drowned out.

A more positive ways of covering the same situation would be this tactful response:

> Although the Beardstown Ladies' Investment Club has already reserved our company training room for Thursday, we would like to suggest that you use our conference room, which seats 25.

No negative words appear in this version. Both approaches yield the primary message of denying the request and offering an alternative, but the positive wording does the better job of building and holding goodwill for the company.

Let's look at some examples of negative and positive sentences. Listen to the tone of each. (The negative words are in italics.)

NEGATIVE WORDING	POSITIVE WORDING
You *failed* to give us the part number of the muffler you ordered.	So that we may get you the muffler you want, will you please check your part number on the enclosed card?
Smoking is *not* permitted anywhere except in the lobby.	Smoking is permitted in the lobby only.
We *regret* to inform you that we must *deny* your request for credit.	For the time being, we can serve you only on a cash basis.
You were *wrong* in your conclusion, for paragraph three of our agreement clearly states . . .	You will agree after reading paragraph three of our agreement that . . .
We *cannot* deliver your order until next Wednesday.	We can deliver your order on Wednesday.

6. People Don't Like Abrasive People

Abrasiveness refers to an irritating manner or tone that sounds pushy or critical. This can hurt the tone of your messages. To determine if you have such a tendency, you might ask yourself the questions in the following Self-Analysis.

Self-Analysis

Do You Have Abrasive Tendencies?

- Are you often critical of others? When you supervise others, do you speak of "straightening them out" or "whipping them into shape"?
- Do you have a strong need to be in control? Must you have almost everything cleared with you?
- Are you quick to rise to the attack, to challenge, to say no?
- Do you have a strong need to debate with others? Do your discussions often become arguments?
- Do you regard yourself as more competent than your peers? Does your behavior let others know that?

Assertiveness and abrasiveness are different. To be assertive is to be pleasantly direct.

The abrasive personality tends to communicate in a manner that can be irritating to others. Try to recognize in yourself how strongly you need to control or dominate other people or tend to have a knee-jerk reaction to things others may say. If you suspect that you do, it is important to make an extra effort to soften the tone of your communications.

Keep in mind that there is a major difference between being abrasive and being assertive. Assertiveness simply means that you express your feelings and observations, normally phrased, in a manner that is nonthreatening to other people. For example, instead of saying to someone, "You don't make any sense," the assertive person says, "I'm having a difficult time understanding what you're saying." Or rather than saying, "Deadbeats like you burn me up," the assertive person might say, "People who consistently make late payments cause us a lot of extra work and lost revenue." Few people get offended by the assertive individual. Indeed, one definition of assertiveness is "being pleasantly direct."

UNDERSTAND THAT ASSERTIVE BEHAVIOR IS NOT AGGRESSIVE BEHAVIOR[10]

Many people confuse assertiveness with aggressiveness. Aggressive behaviors differ in the following ways:

1. *Aggressors communicate from a position of superiority.* Aggressive people feel that they know best or must get their way at almost any cost. They see communication situations as win–lost, meaning that they either get their way or they have lost. And if they lost, someone else wins! The idea of compromise or a decision whereby all parties benefit or win is foreign to them.
2. *Aggressors can be indirect, manipulative, or underhanded.* The aggressive communicator may not be the guy or gal with the big mouth. Sometimes aggressive people use tricks and manipulation such as false emotion or acting false roles designed to get their way. (The TV detective Columbo is actually being aggressive in his questioning by playing dumb and getting people to reveal their guilt!)
3. *Aggressors set themselves up for retaliation.* Aggressive communicators eventually face adversaries. By being less than authentic, they spin webs of deception that get more and more confusing. Like habitual liars, they eventually lose track of what they told whom.
4. *Aggressors use a lot of judgmental or emotionally charged terms for emphasis.* The aggressive communicator thinks that strong language is clear but fails to see how it can create barriers to understanding. Emotional language almost always generates emotionally worded responses.

Assertive behaviors avoid these problems by being honest and authentic. Assertive communicators believe:

1. *In high self-respect for their own ideas and abilities.* Assertive communicators know that they are valuable. Their time, talents, and efforts are to be respected. They take a back seat to no one although they do recognize and respect other peoples' different abilities.
2. *In respect for other people.* They see people as having a wide range of experiences and know that we can all learn something from another person. They know that a organizational title or social status does not guarantee people a right to the best ideas. People need people and can gain much from others.
3. *That win–win solutions can be found for many problems.* The purpose of communication is to create understanding, not to beat out another person. Conflicts or challenges need not be couched in win–lose terms. A fresh perspective or creative twist can often be found to create solutions that leave no one a loser.
4. *That consensus is best created by direct and honest expression of points of view.* The assertive person wins by influencing, listening, and negotiating, not by manipulating.
5. *In honest, open relationships eliminate the desire for retaliation or distrust.* Communication does not get tangled in a web of game-playing. Openness begets openness. People are more comfortable with assertive communicators. They can be trusted.
6. *That emotionally charged language is seldom effective.* Using strong, judgmental words hampers the resolution of problems or creation of understanding. Neutral, descriptive terms are better. They do not turn listeners off.

In addition to assertive and aggressive communication, some people are simply passive. They communicate ineffectively because they do not really care much—they are *apathetic.* Or they have chosen to stay out of a particular discussion.

A FINAL THOUGHT

Customer complaints are opportunities for building customer loyalty. Sure, complainers can be annoying, but they can also be your best friends. They can point out ways to improve and strengthen your business in ways no one else will. That's valuable intelligence for the competitive battlefield. Use it to build customer satisfaction and loyalty.

Summary of Key Ideas

- Customer retention requires positive attitudes toward problem solving but not necessarily an oversimplified "customer is always right" mind-set.

Another Look

Calming Hostile Customers[11]

A hostile, angry reaction usually follows a certain pattern if it is handled skillfully. This pattern is called the hostility curve. Here is what it looks like:

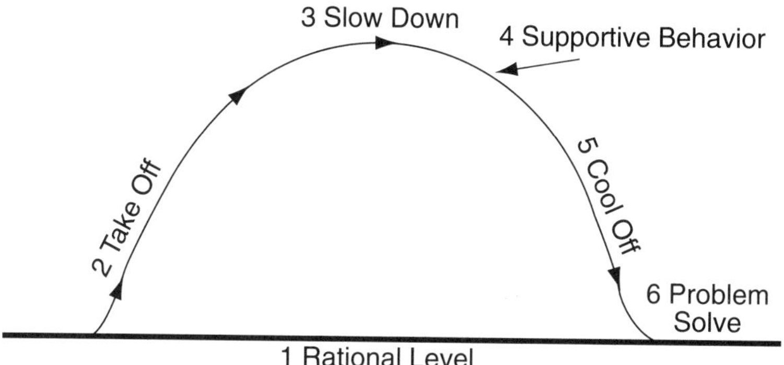

It is important to thoroughly understand each step of the hostility curve:

1. Most persons are reasonable much of the time. They function at a rational level. At this level, you can talk with them about things reasonably.
2. When irritations pile up or a specific incident provokes a person, he or she will *take off,* blowing off steam, possibly becoming abusive, and in general expressing a lot of hostility. Once the person leaves the rational level, there is no use trying to get the person to be "reasonable."
3. This takeoff cannot last forever. If not provoked any further, the hostile person just runs out of steam and begins to *slow down.* He or she may feel embarrassed for making a scene.
4. At this point, the staff member who has been listening to this hostile takeoff can say something. What you say makes a big difference. Say something *supportive,* such as "Things can be awfully frustrating when you're under so much pressure" or "I know this has been an upsetting experience for you." In addition, you must be supportive in your nonverbal behavior. Being supportive does not necessarily mean agreeing, but it does mean letting the other person know that you understand his or her feelings.
5. If you do say something supportive, you usually see the hostile person *cool off.* He or she comes back down to the rational level.
6. Once returned to the rational level, the person and you can begin to problem solve about what caused the anger. Persons are in a

mood to solve problems when they are rational, not when they are at the top of the hostility curve.

Probes

1. Why is it important to help an upset customer cool off before trying to solve the problem?
2. How can you best help him or her through the hostility curve? What specific things could you say? What should you avoid saying or doing?

- The key issue in customer disputes is not who is right or who is wrong, but rather how all parties can cooperate to solve the customer's concerns.
- A customer complaint is an opportunity to cement a relationship and create customer loyalty.
- Recovery skills are necessary to career success and will be regularly used.
- The key skills in recovery involve feeling the customer's "pain," doing all you can to resolve the problem, and then going the extra step via "symbolic atonement."
- After doing your best to deal with a customer problem, it is useful to review the episode and learn from it.
- Handling occasional chronic complainers can best be done by understanding their motives and then getting them to propose an acceptable solution.
- Effective written communication uses human relations principles such as receiver self-interest, receiver-centeredness, and individual treatment using positive information.
- Abrasiveness is a drawback to customer relations, while assertiveness leads to better problem resolution.

Key Terms and Concepts

Abrasiveness
Aggressive behavior
Assertive behavior
"Blanket tone"
Chronic complainers
Customer retention
Hostility curve
Positive and negative wording
Reader self-interest
Receiver-centered and I-centered messages
Recovery skills
"Symbolic atonement"
The three F's: feel, felt, found

Self-Test Questions

1. In customer disputes, who is right or who is wrong is not the key issue. What overriding issue is more important?
2. What are the three important steps needed for *recovery* of the potentially lost customer?
3. What are some things you can do to offer "symbolic atonement" to the dissatisfied customer?
4. What are some of the telltale signs of a chronic complainer?
5. What special customer service techniques can be used when faced with a chronic complainer?
6. What are the three F's? How can they be used to disarm the upset customer?
7. What human relations principles can we apply to improve our written communication?
8. Why should the "blanket tone" be avoided?
9. Compare and contrast assertive versus aggressive behavior.

Application Activity

Defusing and Recovering the Unhappy Customer[12]

Read the following brief case. Then get another person to role play the part of the unhappy customer. Practice responding to his or her concerns in a constructive manner that could lead to recovery of this customer. If possible, videotape your role play and review the tape to identify nonverbal and verbal behaviors.

Before you get into this activity, look carefully at the language used to describe the situation. What problems do you see about the tone? How can you express the viewpoints of the two parties in more constructive terms?

A Hot Traveler and a Hot Motel Manager

The Motel Manager's Story

A fellow from a city several hundred miles away has just checked into your motel. He gives the impression that he is a big-shot government worker. After a short visit to his room, he storms into your office, claiming his air conditioner is faulty. You have recently spent $75 to repair the unit in his room. You are certain that he must have banged it with his fist and that he is responsible for the trouble with the unit. You are not about to let him push you around.

The Traveler's Story

You have just settled into a rather dumpy motel. It is mid-August, and the temperature is 109 degrees. You flip on the switch to the air conditioner; there is a buzz, a hum, and smoke starts to pour out of the vents of the air conditioner. After several bangs with your fist, the smoke vanishes, but the air conditioner will not work. You are hot and tired, and wish you had selected a better motel. At that point, you storm into the motel manager's office, inform him that he runs a cheap, dumpy, and poorly cared-for motel. You demand that he rush immediately to your room and repair your air conditioner.

NOTES

[1]These Office of Consumer Affairs statistics were quoted in *The Customer Service Manager's Handbook of People Power Strategies* (Englewood Cliffs, NJ: Prentice Hall, 1989), p. 3.

[2]J. Mount, "Why Take Sides," *Inc.,* March 1995, 17(3), p. 29.

[3]*Ibid.*

[4]TARP research is cited in J. R. Shannon, "The Components of Customer Service: A New Taxonomy," *Journal of Customer Service in Marketing & Management,* vol. 2(1), 1996, p. 6.

[5]Adapted from "How to Deal with Those Chronic Complainers," *Customer Service Manager's Letter,* September 20, 1989. Published by Prentice Hall Professional Newsletters. The article is based on the work of Dr. Robert Bramson, *Coping with Difficult People* (New York: Dell, 1988).

[6]Excerpted from *Customer Service Manager's Handbook of People Power Strategies* (Englewood Cliffs, NJ: Prentice Hall Professional Newsletters, 1989), pp. 9–10. Reprinted with permission.

[7]Morgan, R. L., *Calming Upset Customers* (Menlo Park, CA: Crisp Publications, 1989), p. 40.

[8]This material is adapted from P. Timm and J. Stead, *Communication Skills for Business and Professions* (Upper Saddle River, NJ: Prentice Hall, Inc., 1996), Chapter 9.

[9]Daniel Starch, *How to Develop Your Executive Ability* (New York: Harper & Row, 1943), p. 154.

[10]P. Timm, *Basics of Oral Communication* (Cincinnati, OH: South-Western Publishing, 1993), pp. 237–8. Reprinted with permission of the publisher.

[11]Adapted from ideas presented in *Teaching Patient Relations in Hospitals: The Hows and Whys* (New York: The American Hospital Association, 1983).

[12]This case originally appeared in P. R. Timm and B. D. Peterson, *People at Work: Human Behavior in Organizations,* 5th ed. (Cincinnati, South-Western College Publishing, 2000), p. 257.

Foundation Skill

4 Exceed Customer Expectations

The Master Key Called E-Plus

Surprising customers with unexpected, positive experiences will do more than anything else to create customer loyalty.

—Retailing pioneer Marshall Field

WHAT YOU'LL LEARN IN THIS CHAPTER

- Psychological theory supports the importance of exceeding customer expectations (creating "E-Plus") to keep customers and build their loyalty.
- Consistently exceeding customer expectations is a powerful key to career success.
- Expectations change and evolve, forcing intelligent businesspeople to adjust and innovate.
- It is important to fish for customer feedback and better assess their expectations.
- Six areas provide the best opportunities for exceeding expectations.
- The best E-Plus ideas come from employees at all levels of the organization.

The Way it Is (or Was)

Walgreen's History of Exceeding Expectations[1]

Charles R. Walgreen Sr. wanted his small Chicago pharmacy to give patrons fast service that would wow them. Every pharmacy at the turn of the century supplied prescriptions. Every pharmacy delivered. But what if his delivered faster?

He decided to use new technology—the telephone—to boost his business. When a nearby customer telephoned an order for some nonprescription goods, Walgreen (1873–1939) slowly repeated both the order and the caller's address out loud. Then Caleb Danner, the store's handyman, after listening, collected and wrapped the items quickly. As Danner darted to the caller's home, Walgreen stretched the conversation for several more minutes, talking about anything under the sun.

This gave Danner time to land at the caller's doorstep, interrupt the phone call, and hand the unsuspecting customer the items ordered minutes before on the phone. Soon, the customer spread the word about the extraordinary service.

The "two-minute stunt" and other innovations helped Walgreen change the face of pharmacies and build what now is America's largest drugstore chain, with more than 2,500 stores and more than $15.3 billion in sales in 1998.

When Walgreen opened his first shop, on the corner of Cottage Grove and Bowen avenues on Chicago's South Side in 1901, drugstores were drab and dimly lit. Customers stopped to find what they needed and left.

Hidden in the back of the store was the pharmacist, working behind a wooden grillwork partition and surrounded by bottles of compounds, a mortar and pestle, and a jar of leeches.

Walgreen saw an opportunity. Most drugstores had small soda fountains. At first, they sold bottled soda water as a health aid. Later, they added flavors, such as lemon, strawberry, and pineapple, and began featuring a small soda fountain apparatus inside their front counter.

Walgreen saw a way to innovate: Why not make the fountains large enough to seat customers at tables and serve treats including ice-cream sodas, phosphates, and sundaes?

Walgreen took action after a shop adjacent to his second drugstore became vacant. He rented the space and cut an archway through the common wall. He installed a 16-foot-long marble-top fountain and a 12-foot mirror bordered by intricate woodwork against the far wall. He also added eight small tables and as many booths.

But Walgreen knew that ice-cream parlors weren't entirely new in the Midwest metropolis. He looked for an edge. He knew customers appreciated high quality. So he developed a private-label ice cream brand for the store that had a higher percentage of butter fat than the ice cream from his suppliers had. His own ice cream was always fresh, because it could be made in minutes in the store's basement.

The soda fountain was a huge success. Customer traffic slumped, however, after summer ended. Walgreen analyzed the situation—he had space to serve ice cream, but people didn't want it when the weather was cold. So he created a new market. Walgreen persuaded his wife, Myrtle, to cook. She fed customers through the winter with a different hot soup, sandwich, and dessert menu every day from Monday to Saturday. It worked, and the fountain stayed busy year round.

The Rio native encouraged his employees to innovate, too. In fact, one of the store's fountain managers in 1922 came up with the fountain's greatest hit —the milkshake. He'd seen how much people liked ice cream, so he created a double-rich chocolate malted milk thickened with three scoops of vanilla ice cream and topped by whipped cream and a cherry. It came with a complimentary package of vanilla cookies. It didn't take long before customers began standing three and four deep at the counter to get their taste of what is now an American classic.

Walgreen came up with new ways and expanded product offerings to boost sales to customers attracted to the store. The Perfume Bar allowed female customers to sample many famous brands while men inspected the cases of cigars and pipe tobaccos. "Concentrations," or striking displays of a specific product, were placed in highly visible areas of the store.

Walgreen also poured energy and time into developing other private-label products—from Sure Death Bug Pizen for killing bedbugs to freshly roasted coffee beans to cold cream. To make sure customers were confident in the house products, the store guaranteed in writing that no item would carry the Walgreen name if it didn't meet high quality standards.

Walgreen also knew customers flocked to sales, but felt that too many sales made a store look cheap. Why not offer everyday discounts on some items? The strategy could work if he bought in bulk. So he persuaded other neighborhood pharmacy owners to pool their purchases of the same products. Walgreen became president of the "Velvet Club" and successfully negotiated with suppliers for lower wholesale prices.

Back then, the concept was so radical that people questioned whether the $1 Gillette razors that sold for 69 cents at Walgreen's were indeed genuine. "Don't be afraid of anything sold at a Walgreen store, for quantity buying permits low prices, and we often sell the equal of gold dollars for less than 100 cents," Walgreen said in the chain's newsletter, The Pepper Pod.

Realizing that customers shopped where they felt most comfortable, Walgreen launched The Pepper Pod in December 1919 to interact more closely with patrons. He made sure the 12-page newsletter included something for everyone. Articles included "Beauty Hints," "Christmas Suggestions," and "Constipation and How to Prevent It."

Customers were thrilled. Walgreen encouraged them to contribute to the publication, thus deepening their loyalty. One article by a customer carried the headline "Germany of Today" in heavy block letters and gave a firsthand account of post–World War I Berlin.

Walgreen never stuck to the tried and true. He wanted his customers to come into a Walgreen store and actually experience the service. To assure it would be good, Walgreen wrote employee manuals on cleanliness, the importance of smiling, and good sales skills.

He even listed ways to handle a preoccupied or worried customer: "Express a real sympathy and understanding in your dealings . . . Don't try to distract his attention from his worries by talking unnecessarily."

Walgreen always wanted employees to make that extra effort. In a book called Set Your Sales for Bigger Earnings, Walgreen provided more tips on how to give the best service.

One illustration showed a smiling, clean-cut salesclerk tying up a stack of items in a neat bundle. The explanation said, "Little extra services are the cheapest kind of advertising that merely takes thought and a few seconds of time!" "Success," Walgreen wrote in the same book, "is doing a thousand little things the right way—doing many of them over and over again."

STAY CLOSE TO YOUR CUSTOMERS

Innovate with the customer constantly in mind. That has been a critical key to many a successful company. As the Walgreen story shows, people's needs, wants, and expectations change, and businesses need to be vigilant in recognizing the opportunities in such changes. Reacting to customer change is good, but being proactive in anticipating change is better.

How can you best anticipate changing customer needs? Staying close to the customer and maintaining an ongoing dialogue is an important key. But just what can you do with the input received from customers? You can use it to best understand their current expectations and, more importantly, to plan approaches that will exceed these expectations. Ultimately, today's customer service success arises from a central theme that is simple to state yet challenging to implement. The underlying theme is:

> You achieve customer satisfaction, retention, and loyalty by exceeding customer expectations in positive ways.

I call this process of exceeding expectations *E-Plus* for short. Research and experience of countless experts points to E-Plus as almost a "master key" to service success. Before we look at the E-Plus formula, and suggest some ways to successfully implement this approach, let's consider some background that can explain the psychology behind E-Plus.

E-Plus is an approach supported by basic psychological theories. It utilizes human nature to create a win–win relationship.

UNDERSTAND WHY CUSTOMERS DO WHAT THEY DO

At a basic psychological level, people are motivated to act in a particular way because they expect either to achieve a gain (reward) or avoid a loss (punishment). Customers are rational people. If a buying experience is positive, they see it as a gain and probably come back; if negative, they regard it as a loss and try to avoid returning. If it's so-so, they'll stay in that zone of indifference discussed in Chapter 2.

The Crucial Role of Customer Expectations

Customers entering into a transaction expect (perhaps unconsciously) to be treated in a particular way. What they expect is often based on their past associations with this business, person, or organization, or ones they see as similar. If they had a good experience in the past, they probably expect something satisfactory. If the last transaction wasn't so positive, they might assume the next one wouldn't be better.

As people enter into a transaction, they harbor certain expectations of how it will be.

Working with people's expectations is difficult for customer service employees because these expectations are *perceptual*. They exist in the mind of our customer. Sometimes they are accurate and rational, sometimes they aren't. And to make matters worse, they are ever-changing. They present a moving, hard-to-define target.

Core Expectations of Products, Services, and the Customer Experience

When people judge the quality of a tangible product, they use fairly objective and somewhat predictable standards. For example, after buying a new automobile, a person is likely to judge its quality by things like:

- Driving and handling characteristics.
- Low frequency of repair (it seldom has to be fixed).
- Appropriate size (it holds the family comfortably).

- A good price relative to its quality (it looks nice but didn't cost an arm and a leg).
- Workmanship (it seems to be well built, nice paint job).

Likewise when we judge the quality of a service (say a house painter's job), we measure it by such standards as:

- The work was done on time (the deadline met).
- The surfaces to be painted were carefully prepared.
- The paints were mixed and applied neatly.
- The painter cleaned up after the job, etc.

The kinds of standards are pretty predictable; they're much the same for each customer.

Customer satisfaction goes beyond the core product. Customers evaluate the entire buying experience.

But evaluating the degree of customer satisfaction goes beyond the core product or service bought. It involves the entire buying *experience*. The standards by which customers measure satisfaction with an experience are more ambiguous.

Self-Analysis

Identifying Core Expectations

Identify your core expectations for the following products or services. What must happen for you to maintain a basic level of customer satisfaction?

Purchase of:

A washing machine.

A computer system.

Repair of your automobile's transmission.

Lawn service for your home.

Copy service for an important report.

A new bicycle.

A dental check-up.

A complete physical.

Carpet cleaning.

Be specific about what you'd consider to be basic expectations.

Customers will be unhappy if their basic expectations are not met.
GEECH © 1993 UNIVERSAL PRESS SYNDICATE.
Reprinted with permission. All rights reserved.

To further complicate matters, expectations differ among organizations or under varying circumstances. When purchasing a tangible product, people expect different treatment from a "high-touch," full-service retailer than they do from a warehouse store. They expect different service from a prestigious law firm than a state automobile license bureau.

For that matter, they probably expect something different from the same store at different times. Perhaps a little less personal attention is anticipated during busy periods (such as during Christmas shopping or end-of-month license plate buying).

Different Expectations from Different Businesses

Suppose you intend to shop at a low-cost, self-service discount store, like Wal-Mart, Kmart, Target, or Fred Meyers. Going into the store, you expect to be treated in a particular way. You do not necessarily expect that the clerk in the clothing department (if you can find one) is an expert in fitting clothing. Nor are you likely to expect that person to be particularly helpful in choosing or color coordinating items. This is not to say that some people who work there would not have these skills, but we probably wouldn't expect them as a general rule.

> Our expectations differ with different types of businesses.

If we simply select clothing items from a rack and take them to a checkout for purchase, we are neither surprised nor particularly disappointed. That's about what we expected and if other aspects of the store are okay (it seems clean and well stocked, for instance), we could be perfectly satisfied.

By contrast, if we were to go to a Nordstrom's, Macy's, or Bloomingdale's full-service department store, or to an exclusive boutique, we would expect a different kind of transaction. We would probably expect to have a salesperson who has considerable expertise in clothing fit, color, and materials. We would realistically expect that service person to assist us as we make our purchases.

When we find situations like these, our expectations are met. Dissatisfaction is probably avoided; we are in that zone of indifference.

The key to exceptional customer satisfaction and a corresponding motivation to return (loyalty), however, lies not in meeting expectations but in *exceeding* them.

When a customer finds his or her expectations exceeded, the likelihood of becoming a repeat customer increases sharply.

One of three situations may arise as we compare our expectations with the service received:

Positive expectations are not fulfilled (the experience is *not as good* as expected). Experience is more negative than expected.	Expectations are met.	Negative expectations are not fulfilled (the experience is *not as bad* as expected). Experience is more positive than expected.

In the condition described in the left box, the customer's experience is as bad as or worse than expected. She's dissatisfied and likely to defect to another provider, if she has a rational alternative. The middle column customer is neither dissatisfied nor particularly motivated to return. This is the zone of indifference we discussed earlier. This customer may or may not return.

In the right column situation, the transaction is better than expected. Either the customer thought it would be pretty good and it was very good, or the customer thought it would not be good but it wasn't as bad as expected. If positive expectations were sufficiently exceeded (or negative ones shown to be unfounded), this customer is a very good candidate for repeat business.

The right column situation is what we'll call an *E-Plus* experience—customer expectations were *exceeded.*

UNDERSTAND WHY E-PLUS LEADS TO CUSTOMER RETENTION

A solid theoretical basis for predicting that the E-Plus (right column) customer will become a repeat customer exists in a theory founded in social psychology called *equity theory.* Psychologist J. Stacy Adams first articu-

E-Plus is based on a theory from social psychology called equity theory.

lated this theory in the mid-1960s.[2] It has stood the test of time to be widely accepted as a predictor of some kinds of human behavior. Here is a quick summary of the theory:

Equity theory starts with the premise that human beings constantly go into and out of various kinds of relationships, ranging from the intimate to the cursory. Long-term relationships like best friendships and families are at one end of the continuum. Brief, even momentary "relationships" like buying something from a convenience store on a cross-country trip or chatting with someone in an airport are at the other end of the continuum. The buyer–seller relationship is germane to this discussion.

We all constantly go into and out of relationships with other people. Some are lasting, some only momentary.

Once in a relationship, even a brief one, people immediately and regularly assess the *relative equity or fairness of their involvement* compared to other people. They check to see if what they give to the relationship balances with what they are getting out of it. A very simple example of a relationship that is out if balance (inequitable) is if you pass another person on a sidewalk and say hello to her but she ignores your greeting and walks on. You've given something and received nothing in return. You'll feel some awkwardness and may wonder what's wrong with her. Is she angry at me? Didn't she hear me? Is she worried about something?

People in relationships constantly monitor the relative fairness of the relationship. Are they getting as much from it as they are giving to it?

A higher-level inequity experience might arise if you invite a new friend and his family to your home for dinner and he never even thanks you, let alone invites you to his place for a meal, or does anything to "rebalance" the relationship.

Initially, much testing of this theory focused on the workplace, where workers' perceptions of fairness (equity) were correlated with certain behaviors. Not surprisingly, studies found that people who were paid less for doing the same work as others, for example, felt a sense of inequity. In my own doctoral research, I found that employees who sensed that their supervisor communicated more often and more positively with other employees in the workgroup felt a clear sense of inequity.[3]

But the theory goes beyond simply citing situations when people may feel inequitably treated. It also predicts what people would do about it. When inequity is sensed, people respond with one or some combination of the following reactions. They may:

- *Ignore or rationalize the inequity.* "He deserves to be treated better than I," "The world isn't fair but I'm not going to fight it," or "I guess he didn't hear me say hello."
- *Demand restitution.* The offended person goes to the boss to demand fairer pay, or the customer wants her money back when product quality is poor.
- *Retaliation.* Employees may tell others about how bad the organization is, do harm to the person seen as the cause of the inequity, or even commit outright sabotage.
- *Withdraw from the relationship.* Employees quit and don't come back.

So far this theory seems to bear out common sense. If we feel we are being unfairly treated, we get upset and usually do something about it. Hence, the unsatisfied participant in a relationship (the customer in our case) is likely to do one of these things. The first two alternatives may give you a chance to patch things up and recover the customer using techniques such as those learned in Chapter 3. But the last two—retaliation or withdrawal—can be devastating. Mrs. Williams, the former Happy Jack's Super Market customer in our Chapter 1 story, did both. She withdrew—quit shopping there—and retaliated by telling her friends, thus starting the negative ripple effects that may have resulted in scores or even hundreds of lost customers or potential customers.

The Positive Side of Equity Theory

Another finding of equity theory predicts this: People who feel that they are receiving *more than they "deserve"* from a transaction also experience a psychological need to restore the balance of fairness. A simple illustration of this is the social pressure you may feel to reciprocate when someone invites you to his or her home for dinner. The relationship remains unbalanced until you rebalance it with a similar kindness: bringing wine or flowers, inviting them to your home, or at least sending a thank-you note.

> People who feel they are getting *more* from the relationship than they put in also feel psychological pressure to restore a balance.

Herein lies the theoretical basis for exceeding customer expectations. By going beyond the expected, you are creating an imbalance that, for many people, requires action on their part to rebalance. The logical options are the opposite of what victims of a negative imbalance feel: They could rationalize or ignore it, of course, but attempts to restore the balance could also take the form of telling others of the positive experience, paying a premium for the goods received, or, in short, becoming a loyal customer.

The challenge, then, is to *create positive imbalances by exceeding customer expectations.* This is the master key called E-Plus. Using this master key requires two kinds of ongoing actions:

1. Continually work to anticipate customer expectations, and then
2. Exceed these expectations.

LEARN TO ANTICIPATE CUSTOMER EXPECTATIONS

Two ways to get a sharper picture of the customer's ever-changing expectations are by fishing for feedback and being receptive to customer input.

Fish for Feedback

Two of the best tools for the feedback fisher are "naive" listening and focus groups. Naive listening is more of an attitude than a strategy. As its name implies, this kind of listening conveys that you don't know—are naive—about what the customer wants. Your task is to get them to explain it to you. Create an atmosphere in which you and your people are cheerfully receptive to customer comments, even—no, *especially*—comments that might not be so pleasant to hear.

Be Receptive to Customer Complaints and Input

The best way to get feedback is to make it easy for people to complain. Let customers know that you are receptive to their problem or concerns. Then provide ways for them to tell you what's on their minds. The use of *open-ended* questions is particularly important. An open-ended question is one that cannot be answered with a simple yes, no, or a one-word response. As such they invariably convey much more information. Restaurant servers who ask, "How else can I make your dinner enjoyable?" get a broader range of responses than one who asks the more common, "Do you need anything else?" or "Is everything okay?"

> The best way to get useful feedback is to create an atmosphere in which your customers can comfortably give suggestions or complain.

Of course, questions aren't just for the complainer. We also need to know what changes we need to make to maintain our customers' ever-changing expectations. Here is where focus groups (discussed in Chapter 2) can come in.

Go fishing for feedback—regularly. Open up the communication channels, and give your customer an opportunity to comment and complain. Remember that at least 63 percent of unhappy customers do not complain, but rather defect to another source of products or services. Of those who do complain *and have their problems addressed—even if not fully resolved,* only 5 percent abandon your business. In a sense, your complaining cus-

Your complaining customer is often your most valuable customer.

tomers are your best customers. Meeting their needs provides an opportunity to solidify a business relationship.

Understanding customer expectations does little good unless you take the second step in the E-Plus process: Regularly develop ways to exceed expectations.

STRIVE TO EXCEED CUSTOMER EXPECTATIONS

Take a look at your responses to the exercise on page 68 where you identified some core expectations about several products or services. Now that you've identified the basics needed to keep you satisfied, what might be some unexpected surprises that you could receive from an enlightened business applying E-Plus? What kinds of little things could make you much more likely to become a loyal customer?

Now let's go back to our fictitious Kmart, Target, or Fred Meyers–type discount store. How might this retailer exceed your expectations—provide some level of service above and beyond what you'd normally expect?

Suppose, for example, you found a person greeting you at the door as you entered the store? Suppose that person welcomed you to the store, and asked if you needed help finding anything in particular? Would that be just a little more than you have expected? Perhaps so, but that is, of course, precisely what Wal-Mart stores have done. By hiring people, often senior citizens on a part-time basis, who serve as greeters, Wal-Mart is exceeding the expectations of many discount store shoppers and, in the process, attracting a lot of customers.

But wait. That idea has been done. Can we take this a step further? Why not get someone to roam the store wearing a special vest that says, "Can I Help You Find Something?" What if that individual looks for customers who appear to be confused or questioning a particular purchase? This individual would have to be exceptionally personable and knowledgeable about the products in the store. Wouldn't that exceed the expectations of most people in a self-service store? That's an example of an E-Plus strategy: consistently doing little things that surprise the customer.

INNOVATE WITH THE SIX E-PLUS OPPORTUNITIES: VISPAC

In my work with clients, I've refined this E-Plus idea to help people get specific by targeting categories of customer expectations. To help remember these categories, we'll use the acronym VISPAC (as in *vis*ible *pac*kaging).

The six categories of E-Plus opportunities (VISPAC) are:

1. Value.
2. Information.
3. Speed.
4. Personality.
5. Add-ons.
6. Convenience.

When customers feel they are getting more than expected in any or all of these six areas, the likelihood of their loyalty increases dramatically. For the next part of this chapter, we will discuss examples of VISPAC.

Value

Value is a function of how long a product lasts.

How can we exceed customer expectations regarding the value—the valuable-ness—of the products we sell? When people think of value, they think of some exceptional products they've owned. Perhaps it's a 15- or 20-year-old Kirby vacuum cleaner, a Ford pickup truck, a Western Auto freezer, or an always accurate and totally reliable tax preparation service. Maybe you have a sweater that dates back a quarter century (I do!), a set of Craftsman tools that never break, or a Timex watch that "takes a lickin' and keeps on tickin'." These products exceed their owners' expectations of value. Buyers feel they got more for their money than they would have ever expected when they purchased these items.

Keep in mind two characteristics of value expectations. First, customers may not fully appreciate the value of something until its long-term quality becomes evident. Conveying E-Plus value to customers may take an extended time to become evident. Second, value is always relative to the price. Indeed, a definition of value is *the quality of a product or service relative to its price.* Some items we buy are throwaways—inexpensive items we don't expect to last. Yet even these can

> Value is defined as quality relative to its cost. Sometimes value does not become apparent until customers become aware of the product's longevity.

exceed expectations if they last a bit longer than we thought they would, or if they cost even less than we would expect.

Sometimes customers need simply to be reminded of the value they are receiving. A City Government may, for example, send information about how tax dollars are being used in the community to show its value. Some discount stores program their computers to show the list prices of products bought alongside their discount prices, thus reinforcing what a good deal the customer received.

To E-Plus a customer you need to create an enhanced *sense* of value. This can be done with such things as *packaging* (e.g., a product seems better if it's nicely wrapped or presented in an attractive box), by *personalizing* the product (e.g., writing a thoughtful note inside a book you give someone), by offering an exceptional *guarantee* (e.g., Craftsman tools are guaranteed for life), or some combination of these.

```
                    BIZMART
366 E. 1300 South                 Store 161
              Orem, UT 84058
SALE                      61853 16104 95630
                  0161 11/12/91 03:58 PM

071402303167
  REFILL,BALLPOINT                     1.50
  MFG. LIST $2.50
072838120007
  MARKER RAZOR PT,                     0.69
  MFG. LIST $1.29
043100171225
  FILLER PAPER PAD                     1.89
  MFG. LIST $2.98
074319240334
  PAD,EASEL 27X34"                     8.79
  MGF LIST $16.00
MEMBER #
PURCHASE ORDER #
                        SUB TOTAL     12.87
                        6.250% TAX     0.80
                        TOTAL        $13.67
                        CHECK         13.67
ACCOUNT NUMBER  00182998
AUTH 9999

                   IPV LN 30380  06913047

 ***********  YOUR PURCHASES  **********

CATALOG LIST PRICES
WOULD HAVE COST YOU              $22.77

BIZMART'S LOW
EVERYDAY PRICES =                $12.87
*******************************
YOU SAVED                         $9.90
*******************************
THAT'S A SAVINGS OF                 43%

    THANK YOU FOR SHOPPING AT BIZMART
```

Information

How can we exceed customer expectations by providing more, better, or clearer information that the customer can use? One of my children had knee surgery a few years ago. Following the surgery, he was assigned a physical therapist who was to teach him how to regain strength in his knees. We expected the therapist to tell him what exercises to do and let it go at that. But the therapist not only explained what exercises he should do but also gave him paper copies illustrating exactly how do them, a thorough demonstration of each workout, and a follow-up phone call a few days later to see how he was doing. These are all little things, of course, but they still represent an E-Plus in my mind.

Today's car salespeople no longer tell you that there is an owner's manual in the glove box you can read. Instead they often spend considerable time with customers explaining all the bells and whistles on the new car. The good ones do this even after the sale is made. This is E-Plus information-giving.

A hospital client I worked with changed the signs in the hospital when it became evident that patients and guests were getting lost and installed color stripes on the corridor floors to direct people to various departments. A cellular phone dealer calls customers to see if they understand how to use all the features and offers to meet to explain them in person.

Often the best opportunities for E-Plus in information-giving are to use nontraditional media. Computer software products are often accompanied by a learning CD or videotape program. Some advertisers like NordicTrack exercise equipment use videos to both sell and demonstrate their products. How can your business give customers more useful information?

Another Look

Alamo E-Plusses with Information[4]

Alamo Rent-A-Car has announced that, due to continued strength of the number of international, multilingual travelers worldwide, the company now offers multilingual rental agreements printed in both English and the renter's language of choice.

Alamo North America locations, which have offered multilingual rental agreements at all U.S. locations since November 1994, maintain a record of each customer's preferred language—French, German, or Spanish—along with other pertinent rental information. When the customer picks up a car, the rental contract is automatically printed in English and their language of choice, making it easier for the customer to read and understand.

Alamo North America also has multilingual capabilities at its two new Canadian locations. In Montreal, rental agreements are printed in French or, if the customer prefers, in English, Spanish, or German. In Vancouver, the rental agreement is printed in English or, if the customer prefers, in French, Spanish, or German.

Alamo Europe provides rental agreements at all its Germany locations in both German and English. In Switzerland, rental agreements in Zurich are printed in German and English, while in Geneva the rental agreements are printed in French and English. Alamo locations in all other countries print rental agreements in English.

Alamo currently serves 15 million travelers a year through 120 locations in the United States and Canada, and 85 international locations in the United Kingdom, Switzerland, Ireland, the Netherlands, Germany, Belgium, Greece, Portugal, and Austria.

Sometimes information and retailing display work together. One example comes from Wal-Mart.[5]

> Pharmacies have changed a lot in the past two decades, but one thing remains constant: the large burden on staff to stock all those little bottles, jars, and boxes in perfectly straight rows in aisle after aisle. Every time a customer picks something up to read the label, you're guaranteed that the thing needs to be straightened or turned so it faces front. It's a lot of work. Not long ago Wal-Mart tried an experiment: it began replacing traditional shelves with a system of bins. Instead of facing a shelf of aspirin bottles, say, the shopper saw a blowup of the aspirin bottle's label. Under that blowup was the bin, into which the aspirin bottles had been dumped.
>
> That made an enormous difference. First, it solved the problem of stocking—a clerk could just roll a trolley of merchandise to the aisle, open the bin, dump in the goods, and move on. No more straight lines. The shoppers liked it better, too—instead of facing a row of bottles with tiny print, they saw a large, easy-to-read version of the label. It was much easier on the eyes, especially for elderly shoppers. Wal-Mart's main concern in making the change was whether shoppers would perceive the bins as being somehow cheaper and lower in quality than the shelves. In fact, just the opposite was true—shoppers said they thought the bins were an upgraded display system—a very elegant solution.

Speed

How can you exceed your customers' expectations with regard to the speed of service? Research of customer turnoffs repeatedly shows that customers dislike having to wait too long for products or services.[6] Across all types of businesses, people want timely responses. My research shows that even when engaged in leisurely dining at an upscale restaurant, people still value timely service.

Federal Express and the other air freight companies promise to deliver your package by 10 o'clock the next morning, but it often arrives by 9 or 9:30. The repair office for a major office equipment company makes it a policy to tell customers precisely when the repair person can be there (thus setting an expectation) and then seeing that the service persons arrive earlier than promised (E-Plus). The reason this works so well in our culture is that people seldom arrive on time. Repair people and delivery services are often notorious for showing up late or not at all! It's a major pet peeve of customers, yet one that can be easily fixed.

> Offering service faster than expected—even when you originally set the expectation—is a powerful form of E-Plus.

Staffing decisions affect speed. At a progressive supermarket, additional cashiers open when more than two customers are in line. Good fast-food restaurants have lunch up almost before you can order it because they staff and train extensively. Are there ways you can give customers a little faster service than they expect?

Marketing researcher Paco Underhill believes that waiting time is the single most important factor in customer satisfaction. When shoppers are made to wait too long in line (or anywhere else), any good impression of overall service plunges. Though not retailers, banks also have to think about how long people wait in line. One bank was about to institute a policy of giving away $5 to any customer who had to wait five minutes or more. After studying the teller lines over the course of two days, Underhill's consulting firm informed the client that this policy would cost it about triple what it had set aside. The bank dropped the plan and went to work on shortening its customers' wait.[7]

Personality

How can you exceed customer expectations with the personality of your people? Every company or organization conveys a personality to its customers. This personality is a composite of countless little behaviors exhibited by the people who work there. Friendliness, courtesy, efficiency, professionalism, and quality are all conveyed via behaviors both verbal and nonverbal.

This dimension of personality is so important that Chapter 5 deals with it at length. For now, the question is, "How can you or your company project positive personality characteristics that exceed customer expectations?"

Often we can E-Plus our customers with our personality.

Add-Ons

How can you exceed customer expectations by giving or selling customers something else they need or appreciate? When a shoe store clerk gives a shoehorn with a pair of new shoes or when he asks if you'd like to try padded inserts or a pair of lifetime guarantee socks, he is using this E-Plus approach. Sometimes add-ons are sold, sometimes given away. Both can be effective. A clerk at a supermarket hands customers a few candy kisses with the receipt, an unexpected thank-you. The hotel check-in desk has a basket of complimentary apples. The paint store salesperson checks to be sure buyers have caulking and sandpaper.

The best kinds of free add-ons are those with high perceived value and low cost to the business. For example, gas stations that give away a free car wash with a fill-up find that such washes cost them about seven cents but have a perceived value of about $3 (which is the price printed on the coupon). Free popcorn or drinks given away with video rentals cost three or four cents but have a much higher perceived value.

> Give away something of perceived value and you tip the equity scale in your favor.

Obviously, this E-Plus opportunity area ties in closely with its marketing counterpart, add-on sales. Marketers have long recognized the value of trying to sell current customers something else so long as you have them here. This can backfire if it's too pushy, but most customers do not resent low-key inquiries about other products. What add-on product or service can you offer your customers?

"If you buy a goldfish, I'll throw in the aardvark."

Add-ons can encourage customer loyalty—if they have perceived value.

HERMAN® is reprinted with permission of Laughingstock Licensing Inc. All rights reserved.

Convenience

How can you exceed customer expectation by making your product or service more convenient than expected? This may be the E-Plus area with the greatest potential in today's efficiency-obsessed culture. Two areas where convenience can be enhanced are in recovery of unhappy customers and in attracting new customers.

Convenience is a great way to E-Plus customers.

Quick-lube auto services have flourished as a response to the need for speed.

The typical response to a customer with a faulty product is, "Bring it in and we'll replace it." But recall our example of how Lexus handled a recall shortly after coming onto the market with their new car. Dealers called customers for an appointment to *pick up* the car and they left a loaner car for the customer. If a customer has to go through the trouble of bringing back a faulty product, you might E-Plus by offering to deliver a replacement.

Twenty years ago if you needed an oil change on your car you'd take it to a service station, leave it for the day, get a ride to work, etc. Today we go to quick-lube shops, drive in, step out of the car, have a cup of coffee in the waiting room, and ten minutes later we are back on the road. That's convenience.

The number one restaurant food in America is pizza. But if you had to go to a pizza restaurant, order your food, and wait 20 minutes for it to be served, I doubt that it would be so popular. It's take-out and pizza delivery services that built the industry.

Customers still face a lot of inconveniences daily. If you can come up with great ideas for E-Plussing in the area of convenience, you have a strong competitive advantage. Shopping via the Internet is one obvious approach that is now being tapped. How can you make things more convenient for your customers?

Convenience is one of the most promising E-Plus opportunity areas because so much of what customers face today is inconvenient.

RECOGNIZE WHERE GOOD E-PLUS IDEAS COME FROM

These ideas are, of course, simply illustrative. The possibilities for E-Plus are quite literally unlimited. E-Plus organizations constantly fish for new "little things" that can and will make huge differences. E-Plus requires constant incremental improvements. Little improvements, little innovations lead to a payoff that is enormous. E-Plus really is the master key for customer satisfaction and retention. If you're not thinking E-Plus, your competition may be.

"Don't bother undressing. I'll turn up the power."

Convenience is a powerful E-Plus opportunity area.

HERMAN® is reprinted with permission of Laughingstock Licensing Inc. All rights reserved.

To get a constant flow of new E-Plus ideas, ask employees at all levels of the organization to apply creativity. Work to create an environment in which new ideas are tried and innocent mistakes are not punished. Have supervisors or team leaders get together regularly to brainstorm new ideas. Then reward the best ideas with recognition and possibly prizes. The result of this process (which is described in more detail in Chapter 7) is a lively, vibrant, evolving organization with a strong and competitive advantage that cannot be duplicated by your competition.

Activity

E-Plus Brainstorming

Working in teams of five to ten people, imagine yourself in the role of a business you are familiar with (retailing, health care, insurance office, hotel/restaurant, public utility, repair shop, etc.). Using the worksheets found on pages 83 through 88, brainstorm E-Plus ideas that might be useful. Be careful not to be overly judgmental as you come up with ideas. The wilder the better in many cases. You can then go back and refine the group's best ideas.

If you decide to fish for ideas in the personality category, read Chapter 5 before completing this assignment.

VISPAC Worksheet #1

VALUE. E-Plus your customers by creating a perception of value that exceeds their expectations. List ideas for clarifying or presenting an enhanced sense of value in your product or service. Consider such things as various payment options, clarity of billing so that the customer understands costs of different services, and highlighting any discounts given. Remember that value is a relationship of *quality compared to cost.* Consider such things as guarantees, packaging, etc.

After brainstorming possible ideas, put a check in the box next to ideas for further consideration.

❑

❑

❑

❑

❑

❑

❑

❑

The best idea for implementation now is:

VISPAC Worksheet #2

INFORMATION. E-Plus your customers with more, better, or different information than they expect. Consider the possibility of using different media. List ideas for clarifying, improving, or presenting additional information customers may find useful as they use the product or service.

After brainstorming possible ideas, put a check in the box next to ideas for further consideration.

❑

❑

❑

❑

❑

❑

❑

❑

The best idea for implementation now is:

VISPAC Worksheet #3

SPEED. E-Plus your customers by exceeding customer expectations about your efficiency or response times. List ideas for reducing delays or providing faster service than customers might anticipate. Remember that slow service is the number-one complaint of customers in almost every type of business. Your task is to be faster and/or to clarify realistic expectations for customers.

After brainstorming possible ideas, put a check in the box next to ideas for further consideration.

- ❑
- ❑
- ❑
- ❑
- ❑
- ❑
- ❑
- ❑

The best idea for implementation now is:

VISPAC Worksheet #4

PERSONALITY. E-Plus your customers by conveying pleasant, attentive, personable service that exceeds what they may expect. Consider any small verbal or nonverbal "message" you may be sending out. Include possible dialogue ideas for telephone or personal visitors.

After brainstorming possible ideas, put a check in the box next to ideas for further consideration.

- ❑
- ❑
- ❑
- ❑
- ❑
- ❑
- ❑
- ❑

The best idea for implementation now is:

VISPAC Worksheet #5

ADD-ONs. E-Plus your customers by giving or selling them something additional. List ideas for surprising them with a small gift or premium. Consider add-on products they may benefit from or need to make the best use of something they've already purchased.

After brainstorming possible ideas, put a check in the box next to ideas for further consideration.

- ❑
- ❑
- ❑
- ❑
- ❑
- ❑
- ❑
- ❑

The best idea for implementation now is:

VISPAC Worksheet #6

CONVENIENCE. E-Plus your customers by making life easier for them than they expected. List ideas for enhancing their experience with your product or service. Consider such things as free delivery, in-home or in-office services, your handling follow-up details, etc.

After brainstorming possible ideas, put a check in the box next to ideas for further consideration.

- ❑
- ❑
- ❑
- ❑
- ❑
- ❑
- ❑
- ❑

The best idea for implementation now is:

Another Look

Legacy Audio

A recent *Wall Street Journal* article describes a small but highly successful company that "makes stereo speakers for snobs." Legacy Audio charges as much as $12,500 for a pair of it's exceptionally high-quality speakers. The company's founders, Jake Albright and Bill Dudleston, do a great job of listening to their customers and meeting their needs, as described in this excerpt:[7]

> From marketing to manufacturing to shipping, every aspect of the business was organized around the perceived customer's point of view.
>
> To build trust for Legacy's unfamiliar name, Bill designed ads showing the grandfatherly Jake in his woodworking apron—the master craftsman from central casting. When a customer called for a catalog on the toll-free line, the details of the call were added to a homegrown database. Each time a potential customer called back—audiophiles ask lots of questions—a sales agent called up details of previous conversations to the screen.
>
> As the company grew, Bill staffed the phone lines with people from the shop or the engineering lab, reckoning that hands-on experience would make the pitch more convincing. Anyone considering a purchase was invited to fax in a room layout; discussing the particulars of upholstery and floor finishes created a feeling of intimacy. Bill figured that no major competitor could ever match that level of customer interaction. "That's how you box people out of your market," he says.
>
> To make the most of the magic moment when the delivery truck arrived at a customer's home, Legacy created a fancy wooden shipping crate that prevented dings and scratches (while ending the need for environmentally incorrect plastic peanuts; such are the delicacies of selling to a high-brow crowd).
>
> And despite his love of the technical (and his degrees in math and physics), Bill insisted that every unit be tested not only electronically but by a customer's only method: listening. Over and over today, speakers are put through their paces with an extraordinary falsetto passage by the R&B artist Aaron Neville, "a complete frequency sweep," Bill says, "in four seconds."

Probes . . .

1. How does Legacy Audio apply the E-Plus concepts described in this chapter?
2. Would such attention to customers work for any kind of business?

A Summary of Key Ideas

- Consistently exceeding customer expectations is a powerful key to career success.
- A theory from social psychology called equity theory supports the importance of exceeding customer expectations (creating "E-Plus") to keep customers and build their loyalty.
- When people feel they are getting more than they "deserve" from a relationship, they feel subtle pressures to rebalance the relationship by giving more to it.
- Ever-changing expectations force intelligent businesspeople to constantly adjust and innovate.
- Fishing for customer feedback helps us better assess expectations.
- Six areas provide the best opportunities for exceeding expectations: value, information, speed, personality, add-ons, and convenience.
- The best E-Plus ideas emerge from alert, innovative people at any level in the organization.

Key Terms and Concepts

Customer expectations
"E-Plus"
Equity theory
Exceeding customer expectations
"Fish" for customer feedback
Inequity
Open-ended questions
The buying experience
Value
VISPAC

Self-Test Questions

1. How does the social psychology theory of equity apply to customer service? What are some common reactions to perceived inequity?
2. What are some effective ways to encourage your employees to fish for new customer service ideas?
3. What role does convenience play in satisfying customers?
4. What are add-ons? List several examples.
5. In what kinds of ways can a company use information to exceed their customers' expectations?
6. What is the definition of value when applied to customer service?
7. What are two ways to anticipate the customer's ever-changing expectations?

NOTES

[1]David Chung, "Retailer Charles R. Walgreen Sr.: His Innovations Helped Build Nation's Biggest Drugstore Chain," Copyright © 1998 *Investors Business Daily,* used with permission of IBD. Transmitted July 22, 1999 on AOL.

[2]The basic premises of equity theory can be found in J. S. Adams, "Toward an Understanding of Inequity," *Journal of Abnormal and Social Psychology,* 67 (1963): 422–36. Later studies are summarized in L. Berkowitz and E. Walster (eds.), *Advances in Experimental Social Psychology,* vol. 9 (New York: Academic Press, 1976).

[3]Paul Roy Timm, "Effects of Inequity in Supervisory Communication Behavior on Subordinates in Clerical Workgroups," unpublished doctoral dissertation, Florida State University, © 1977.

[4]Transmitted via America Online. Fort Lauderdale, FL, June 9, 1995 PRNewswire.

[5]Paco Underhill, "What Shoppers Want," *Inc.,* July, 1999, p. 78.

[6]Ibid., p. 76

[7]T. Petzinger, "Audio Legacy Shows Value of Feedback in Speaker Sales," *Wall Street Journal,* August 8, 1996, p. B1.

Foundation Skill

5

Use Behaviors That Win Customer Loyalty

It's What You *Do*

> *. . . if a man offend not in word, the same is a perfect man, and able also to bridle the whole body. Behold, we put bits in horse's mouths, that they may obey us; and we turn about their whole body.*
>
> —*The Bible* (James 3:2–3)

WHAT YOU'LL LEARN IN THIS CHAPTER

- Behavior is what people do, and much of it is conveyed via verbal or nonverbal communication.
- Individual actions, as well as organizational behaviors, convey messages to customers that may be productive or counterproductive to their perception of service received.
- Any behaviors (or lack of behaviors) can communicate; the receiver of the message (e.g., the customer) determines what the message means.
- Exceeding expectations in the area of personality depends on both individual actions and the organization's behaviors or culture.

- The role of communication in projecting behavior and two critical rules of communicating.
- Fifteen specific behaviors can exceed customer expectations in the area of individual personality.
- Seven actions convey the organization's personality (culture) to customers.

The Way It Is

Recognize That Anything Can Convey a Message

Humorist Dave Berry tells this story:[1]

> Joe [my attorney] has a client whom I'll call Charles, a mild-mannered financial officer who has never been in any kind of trouble. One evening Charles was driving home from work on the New England Thruway and came to a toll plaza. When his turn came, he pulled up to the booth and held out his $1.25. At this point, the toll taker pulled out what Charles described as "the biggest pile of one-dollar bills I have ever seen," and started slowly counting them. A minute went by. A line of cars formed behind Charles. *Another* minute went by. Charles sat there, looking in disbelief at the toll taker, who apparently planned to continue counting the entire pile of bills, and then, who knows, maybe read *War and Peace.* In the lengthening line behind Charles, more people were honking, shouting, gesturing, possibly rummaging through their glove compartments for firearms.
>
> Finally Charles, despite being mild-mannered, did a bad thing. In fact he did *three* bad things: (1) He made an explicit, non–toll-related suggestion to the toll taker; (2) he threw his $1.25 into the booth; and (3) he drove away.
>
> He did not get far, of course. Western Civilization did not get where it is today by tolerating this kind of flagrant disregard of toll procedures. Charles was swiftly apprehended by two police cars, which escorted him to the police station, where he called Joe, who managed to keep him out of prison through the shrewd legal maneuver of telling him to pay the $50 fine.

Behavior is, of course, what people do. It is conveyed to others via both verbal and nonverbal communication. Our friend the toll taker used no verbal communication (no words were spoken) but still communicated loud and clear a wide range of messages, most of which said he didn't care about his customer.

In less blatant cases, we all occasionally communicate the "wrong" message with our nonverbal behaviors. A salesperson who fails to greet a customer, a fellow worker who shows up late, a repair person who leaves a mess—all communicate something. Two important rules of communication are:

1. Anything can and will communicate.
2. The receiver of the message determines what it "means."

The remainder of this chapter looks at some of the kinds of behaviors—of individuals and of organizations—that convey meaning to customers. This is by no means an exhaustive list of all possible behaviors, but it does reflect some of the more common ones that associate closely with customer satisfaction.

> Any behaviors can, and often will, communicate meaning to our customers.

USE BEHAVIORS AND PERSONALITY FACTORS TO E-PLUS CUSTOMERS

In Chapter 4, we discussed exceeding expectations (we called it E-Plus) and we identified six opportunity areas for E-Plus: value, information, speed, *personality,* add-ons, and convenience. Now is the time to look more closely at personality, a powerful way to create E-Plus experiences for customers.

Each customer encounters two interrelated personalities: the personality of the individual who serves the customer and the overall personality of the organization. This organizational personality is a reflection of the company's "culture." Culture is a composite of many factors that strengthen and reinforce individual behavior. If a company is a fun place to work, its people convey a sense of enjoyment to customers. If the culture is more formal (say, as in a law firm or other professional services office), it is reinforced by employee behaviors and other organizational factors (which will be discussed later in this chapter).

Wal-Mart founder Sam Walton understood organizational behavior when he taught that "People will treat your customers the way you [meaning managers] treat your people." Enthusiasm, comradeship, a sense of enjoyment, and humor quickly become evident to customers. Southwest Airlines, which has a culture of informality and fun at work, projects an organizational personality very different from many of its competitors. This personality has been useful both in attracting customers and attracting employees who enjoy working in such an atmosphere. Indeed, research studies of the best companies to work for consistently identify "having fun" as a critically important criterion.

KNOW WHICH INDIVIDUAL BEHAVIORS CAN CONVEY PERSONALITY

Often the subtlest behaviors can convey the most powerful messages to customers. The little things mean everything. This chapter looks at 15 individual behaviors that, taken together, project personality. As you become aware of these, you'll quickly recognize E-Plus opportunities in each. Awareness alone can improve service, yet many employees are essentially clueless as to the impact of these kinds of behaviors.[2]

1. Greet Customers Like Guests

Woody Allen once said that 80 percent of success is just showing up. In customer service, 80 percent of success is just treating the customer like a guest who just showed up. When guests come to your home, you greet them, right? You say, "Hello" or "Hi there." Yet we've all been totally ignored by service people in some businesses. A friendly greeting is one of those little things that mean a lot.

Initiate Conversation Promptly

> The failure to be greeted creates stress in a customer.

Studies have clocked the number of seconds people had to wait to be greeted in several businesses. Researchers then asked customers how long they'd been waiting. In every case, the customer's estimate of the time elapsed was much longer than the actual time. A customer waiting 30 or 40 seconds often feels like it's been three or four minutes! Time drags when you're being ignored.

A prompt greeting reduces customer stress. Why would customers feel stress? Remember, they are on unfamiliar turf. They are likely to feel somewhat uncomfortable. You work there every day; they are just visiting. A prompt, friendly greeting starts to relax the customer and greases the wheels of smooth service.

Speak Up

Verbally greet customers within 10 seconds of the time they come into your store or approach your work location. Even if you are busy with another customer or on the phone, pause to say hello and let them know that you'll be ready to help them soon.

Get the Customer Committed

Did you ever wonder why some fast-food restaurants send a clerk out to jot down your order while you are waiting in line? Think about it. The person writes what you want on a slip of paper and gives it back to you to present at the cash register where the order is called out. Why is this done? It is simply a way of getting the customer committed. If no one greeted you or wrote your order, you might be more likely to leave before ordering. Psychologically, you feel like you've "ordered" so you stay in line and follow through with your lunch purchase.

So greet customers promptly, verbally if possible, and try to commit them as soon as they come into your business or work area.

2. Break the Ice

The best way to start a conversation depends on what customers need. In many cases, especially in retail stores, customers need first to be reassured that this is a "nice friendly place" to do business. They need to dispel worries about being high-pressured into buying. To do so, use a nonthreatening icebreaker. Often customers want to browse, get the feel of the place before they commit to doing business.

The best icebreaker for the browser can be an off-topic, friendly comment. Some good ones might be:

- *A compliment.* "That's a very sharp tie you're wearing." "Your children are sure cute. How old are they?"
- *Weather-related or local interest comments.* "Isn't this sunshine just beautiful?" "Some snowfall, isn't it?" "How about those Bulls last night?"
- *Small talk.* Look for cues about one's interests in sports, jobs, mutual acquaintances, past experiences, etc. Then initiate a relevant comment.

If browsing customers seem to be focusing attention on a product (holding several shirts or looking at a particular line of products), they can be reclassified as "focused shoppers."

The best icebreaker for the focused shopper is specific to the buying decision. It may:

- *Anticipate the customer's questions.* "What size are you looking for, sir?" "Can I help you select a —?"
- *Provide additional information.* "Those shirts are all 25 percent off today." "We have additional — in the stockroom."
- *Offer a suggestion or recommendation.* "Those striped suits are really popular this season." "If you need help with measurements, our estimators can figure out what you need."

Be attentive to customers' needs. Give them time to browse if that's what they need, but be responsive in helping them to make a buying decision when they are ready to buy. Retail industry research shows that 60 to 80 percent of all shopping decisions are made in the store at the point of sale.[3] This is precisely the point where customers come face-to-face with your personality.

> Learn what "icebreaker" lines work best for different kinds of customers.

In nonretailing organizations, use a friendly, sincere expression of willingness to serve. Reassure customers that you can help them. Ask questions to identify their needs, concerns, or problems.

3. Compliment Freely and Sincerely

It takes only a second to say something nice to a person, and the comment can add enormous goodwill. Say something complimentary to your internal and external customers. Here is safe ground for sincere compliments:

- *Some article of clothing or accessories they are wearing.* "I like that tie!" "That's a beautiful sweater you have on." "Those shoes look really comfortable. I've been looking for some like that." "What a beautiful necklace."
- *Their children.* "Your little boy is really cute." "How old is your daughter? She's beautiful." "He looks like a bright young man."
- *Their behavior.* "Thanks for waiting. You've been very patient." "I noticed you checking the —. You're a careful shopper." "Thanks for your friendly smile."
- *Something they own.* "I like your car. What year is it?" "I noticed your championship ring. Did you play on that team?"

To get yourself in the habit of complimenting, try this: Set a goal to give 10 sincere compliments each day. Make it a habit and you'll see a sharp increase in your personal popularity. People love to be complimented. And, of course, complimenting internal customers (e.g., coworkers) can help create a supportive and pleasant work climate.

> Many people are hesitant to give compliments. People love to receive a sincere compliment. Make it a habit to give compliments.

4. Call People by Name

A person's name is his or her favorite sound. We appreciate it when people make the effort to find out and use our names in addressing us. When appropriate, introduce yourself to customers and ask their names. If this isn't appropriate (such as when you are waiting on a line of customers), you can often get the customer's name from a check, credit card, order form, or other paperwork.

> Use your customer's name if given the opportunity. It builds the relationship.

But don't be overly familiar too quickly. You are normally safe calling people "Mr. Smith" or "Ms. Jones" but may be seen as rude if you call them Homer and Marge. (This is especially true when younger employees are dealing with older customers.) Better to err on the side of being too formal. If people prefer first-name address, they'll tell you so.

5. Talk to Customers with Your Eyes

Even in situations when you may not be able to say hello out loud or give undivided attention to a customer right away, you can make eye contact. Simply looking at your customer tells them much about your willingness to serve. Eye contact creates a bond between you and the customer. It conveys your interest in communicating further. Here is a personal example when the wrong message was conveyed:

> Establishing eye contact can convey a message that you are willing to serve them.

> I went into a very small watch repair shop. The shop was no more than ten feet square. The proprietor was a real expert at repairing timepieces and his prices were good. As I squeezed into his tiny shop he was serving another customer. I stood not more than five feet away from him for several minutes without his ever acknowledging me. It got pretty uncomfortable. Once he finished with the customer ahead of me he was attentive and effective, but he ran a real risk of losing me before he got a chance to show me what he could do—simply because it felt awkward standing there without being acknowledged. All he would have needed to do is say hello and let me know that he would be with me momentarily.

As with your greeting, the timing is important. The ten-second rule also applies here. Make eye contact with a customer within ten seconds, even if you are busy with another person.

As with the spoken greeting, you don't have to interrupt what you are doing with another customer. Just a pause and a quick look captures new customers into an obligation to deal with you further, greatly reducing the chance that they will feel ignored and leave.

When working with customers, be sensitive to *how* you look at them. Communication expert Bert Decker[4] says that the three "I's" of eye communication are intimacy, intimidation, and involvement. Intimacy (like when we're expressing love) and intimidation (when we want to exert power) are both communicated by looking at another person for a long period—from 10 seconds to a minute or more.

But most communication in business settings calls for Decker's third I—involvement. In our culture, people create involvement by looking at the other person for five- to ten-second periods before looking away briefly. This is generally comfortable for

> Eye contact, or lack of it, conveys powerful messages to customers.

people. If you look away more often than that, you may be seen as "shifty" or suspicious; if you lock in eye contact for longer, it feels like intimidation or intimacy.

6. Ask Often: "How'm I Doing?"

Legendary politician and former New York City Mayor Ed Koch would constantly ask his constituents, "How 'm I doing?" The phrase became his tag line. There is some evidence that he even listened to their answers. After all, he survived as mayor of the Big Apple for many years. We can learn something from the Koch question.

Businesses need to ask that question in as many ways as possible. In addition to more formalized measurement and feedback systems, employees need to demonstrate an attitude of receptiveness. Being receptive to the comments and criticisms of people is challenging and, at times, frustrating. It takes a lot of courage not only to accept criticism but to actually request it!

> An attitude of receptiveness is revealed by a willingness to ask questions—and to listen to the answers.

As we discussed in Chapter 3, some of your best ideas come from the correction others give you.

7. Listen with More Than Your Ears

Since so few people are really good listeners, this skill provides an excellent E-Plus opportunity. There is no such thing as an unpopular listener. Almost everyone becomes more interesting when he stops talking and starts listening. Pay attention to your talk–listen ratio. Are you giving the customer at least equal time?

To be a better listener, use these ideas:

- *Judge the content* of what people are saying, *not the way they are saying it.* Customers may not have the "right" words, but they know what they need better than anyone.
- *Hold your fire.* Don't jump to make judgments before your customer has finished talking.
- *Work at listening.* Maintain eye contact and discipline yourself to listen to what is being said. Tune out those thoughts that get you thinking about something else.
- *Resist distractions.* Make the customer the center of your attention.
- *Seek clarification* from customers so that you fully understand their needs. Do this in a nonthreatening way, using sincere, open-ended questions.

8. Say Please and Thank You

At the risk of sounding like one of those books about "things I learned in kindergarten," *be polite.* It may seem old-fashioned and some customers may not be as polite to you, but that's not *their* job. In a recent "Dear Abby" column, the writer complained about salespeople who said "There you go" to conclude a transaction. That kind of comment is not an appropriate substitute for thanking the customer.

"Please" and "thank you" are powerful phrases for building customer rapport and creating customer loyalty. They are easy to say and well worth the effort.

9. Reassure the Customer's Decision to Do Business with You

Buyer's remorse can set in pretty fast, especially when people make a large purchase. At the time of sale, you can inoculate customers against remorse by reassuring them that they've made a good purchasing decision.

Offer phrases like, "I'm sure you'll get many hours of enjoyment out of this," or "Your family will love it." These reassure and strengthen buyers' resolve to follow through with the purchase and, as importantly, feel good about it.

A government agency staffer might say, "I'll bet you're glad that's over with for another year," or "I'll handle the renewal—you've done all that is necessary."

A powerful tool for reassuring is the telephone. One consulting approach for bank executives shows how important customer calls can be. As part of a training session, the executives develop a simple script and immediately go to the phones to call some of their customers. The conversation goes something like this:

> Hello, I'm Chris Wilson from Major Bank. I just wanted to call to let you know that we appreciate your business and would be interested in any suggestions you might have for additional ways we could serve you.

That's about it. Then they let the customer talk. The results: Customers are astounded that their banker would actually call and wasn't trying to sell anything! The image of the bank's service goes up sharply.

10. Smile

As the adage goes, "You are not dressed for work until you put on a smile." Or, as a more cynical person might say, "Smile. It makes people wonder what you've been up to." But more importantly, it tells customers that they came to the right place and are on friendly grounds.

Keep in mind that a smile originates in two places: the mouth and the eyes. A lips-only version looks pasted on, insincere. It's like saying "cheese" when being photographed. It doesn't fool anyone. In fact it might scare them away!

The eyes, however, are the windows to the soul and tell the truth about your feelings toward people. So smile with your eyes and your mouth. Let your face show that you're glad your guest arrived.

A genuine smile originates in the eyes, not the mouth.

Some people smile more readily than others.
July 19, 1994, The Wall Street Journal—Permission, Cartoon Features Syndicate

Now, in fairness, some people smile more readily than others. For some a more serious facial expression is comfortable and natural. But in American culture, a smile is both expected and appreciated when one is meeting people. If you don't smile spontaneously, practice it. It need not be a Cheshire Cat, ear-to-ear grin (in fact that may *really* get people wondering about you) but just a pleasant, natural smile. Look too at your eyebrows. Some people knit their brows and appear to be scowling, even when they don't intend to. Look at yourself in the mirror. Work on facial expression as an actor might.

11. Use Good Telephone Techniques

Remember that your telephone customer can't see you and adjust your behaviors accordingly.

Telephone use calls for some special behaviors, especially if your only contact with customers is via the phone. A key to successful phone use is to simply *remember that your customer cannot see you.* Your challenge is to make up for all that lost nonverbal communication by using your voice effectively. Chapter 8 goes into depth about telephone techniques, but for now, let's review a few key behaviors:

- *Give the caller your name.* Let the caller know who you are just as you would in a face-to-face situation (via a name tag or desk plaque).
- *Smile into the phone.* Somehow people can hear a smile over the phone! Some telephone pros place a mirror in front of them while they're on the phone to remind then that facial expression can transmit through the wires.
- *Keep your caller informed.* If you need to look up information, tell the customer what you are doing. Don't leave them holding a dead phone with no clue as to whether you are still with them.
- *Invite the caller to get to the point.* Use questions such as, "How can I assist you today?" or "What can I do for you?"
- *Commit to requests of the caller.* Tell the caller specifically what you will do and when you will get back to them. "I'll check on this billing problem and get back to you by five this afternoon, okay?"
- *Thank the caller.* This lets the caller know when the conversation is over.
- *Let your voice fluctuate in tone, rate, and loudness.* You hold people's attention by putting a little life into your voice. Express honest reactions in expressive ways. Let your voice tones be natural and friendly.
- *Use hold carefully.* People hate being put on hold. When it's necessary, explain why and break in periodically to let them know they haven't been forgotten. If what you're doing takes longer than a few minutes, ask the caller if you can call them back. *Write down your commitment to call back and don't miss it.*
- *Use friendly, tactful words.* Never accuse the customer of anything; never convey that a customer's request is an imposition.[5]

12. Watch Your Timing

Nothing impresses so significantly as immediate follow-through. Successful salespeople follow up with customers (usually by phone) to see that their purchases are satisfactory. Some salespeople do this occasionally when they have a little spare time; the more successful do it regularly at scheduled times. Likewise, the best customer-oriented people outside of sales make commitments to customers and *always follow up.*

A simple form can help you follow up with customers and save commitments from dropping through the cracks. Make up your form in a notebook or on separate sheets. Include these four columns:

Customer Follow-Up Form

Date	Commitment (Name, Phone Number,What You Promised)	Due	Done

13. Reach Out and Touch Them

Physical touch is a powerful form of communication. Take an opportunity to shake hands with customers or even pat them on the back, if appropriate.

A study of bank tellers shows the power of touch. Tellers were taught to place change in the hand of the customer rather than place it on the counter. Researchers found that customer perceptions of the bank rose sharply among customers who had been touched. In a similar study, servers who touched their restaurant customers when serving the food, making change, or giving a receipt found their tips increased dramatically.

Among internal customers and coworkers, a literal pat on the back can build instant rapport. But don't overdo it; some people resent people who seem too "touchy-feely." Recognize different preferences; try touching behavior but be willing to adjust if the person seems uncomfortable or ill at ease. And, of course, the key word is appropriateness. Never touch a person in a manner that could be interpreted as overly intimate or having sexual overtones.

> Appropriate touching is a powerful form of communication. But be sure it is socially and personally acceptable.

14. Enjoy People and Their Diversity

J. D. Salinger said, "I am a kind of paranoid in reverse. I suspect people of plotting to make me happy." With an attitude like that we'd look forward to every meeting with every customer. Of course, we quickly learn that some customers do not seem to be plotting to make us happy. Most are very pleasant. Some are unusual. A few are downright difficult.

Every person is different; each has a unique personality. But the kind of people who tend to bug us the most are the ones who are *not like us*. Accept this diversity and learn to enjoy it. Know that peoples' needs are basically the same at some level and that treating them as guests creates the most goodwill, most of the time.

> Try to keep your mind void of excessive criticism or cynicism.

Work on Verbal Discipline

Confine your "self-talk" (those internal conversations in your mind) and your comments to others to focus on the positive, and avoid being judgmental. Instead of saying, "Can you believe that ugly dress on that lady?" avoid any comment, or say, in a nonjudgmental way, "She dresses interestingly." Instead of saying, "This guy will nickel and dime me to death," say, "This customer is very cost-conscious."

At times you have to force yourself to avoid the negative and judgmental, but accept the challenge and you can make a game out of it. Sincerely try for one full day to *avoid saying anything negative or judgmental* about another person. If you make it through the day, shoot for another day. Verbal discipline can become a habit that pays off. You'll find yourself enjoying people more.

15. Maintain a Positive Attitude about Selling

Everyone is in sales, regardless of job title.

Many people hold some imagined negative stereotype about selling. Customer contact people sometimes refuse to call themselves salespeople, preferring terms like "associate" or even "consultant." Yet everyone is in sales to some degree. We constantly sell (convince, persuade, whatever term you prefer) other people on ourselves, our products or services, and our company.

Like any profession, selling requires professional skills and attitudes. But often these skills and attitudes are different than one might think. For example, it surprises some people to find that you do not need to be an extrovert to be successful at selling. Quiet, thoughtful people are often very successful. A quiet self-confidence is more important than "techniques." Elwood Chapman, who has trained thousands of salespeople, said that you are likely to be good at sales if you agree with statements like these:[6]

- *I can convert strangers into friends quickly and easily.*
- *I can attract and hold the attention of others even when I have not met them.*
- *I love new situations.*
- *I'm intrigued by the psychology of meeting and building a good relationship with someone I do not know.*
- *I would enjoy making a sales presentation to a group of executives.*
- *When dressed for the occasion, I have great confidence in myself.*
- *I do not mind using the telephone to make appointments with people I don't know.*
- *I enjoy solving problems.*
- *Most of the time, I feel secure.*

There is certainly nothing demeaning about selling a product or service.

Self-Analysis

How Do You Measure Up?

We've discussed the following list of 15 individual behaviors in this chapter. Be completely honest in evaluating how well you do with each. There is nothing wrong with admitting shortcomings; indeed it is far more damaging to deny them. After rating yourself on the scale, go back through the list and circle the plus (+) or minus (–) to indicate how you *feel* about your response. If you are comfortable with your answer, circle the (+). If you wish you could honestly answer otherwise, circle the (–).

The scale meanings:

N = never O= occasionally S= sometimes
M= most of the time A = always

	N	O	S	M	A	+	–
1. I greet all customers like guests.	N	O	S	M	A	+	–
2. I use appropriate ice-breakers.	N	O	S	M	A	+	–
3. I compliment people freely and often.	N	O	S	M	A	+	–
4. I call customers by their name.	N	O	S	M	A	+	–
5. I make and maintain eye contact with customers.	N	O	S	M	A	+	–
6. I often ask for feedback to find out how I'm doing.	N	O	S	M	A	+	–
7. I listen well.	N	O	S	M	A	+	–
8. I always say "please" and "thank you."	N	O	S	M	A	+	–
9. I reassure customer's decisions to do business with me.	N	O	S	M	A	+	–
10. I smile freely and often.	N	O	S	M	A	+	–
11. I know and use good telephone techniques.	N	O	S	M	A	+	–
12. I am always sensitive to timing and follow up with customers.	N	O	S	M	A	+	–
13. I appropriately touch customers when possible.	N	O	S	M	A	+	–

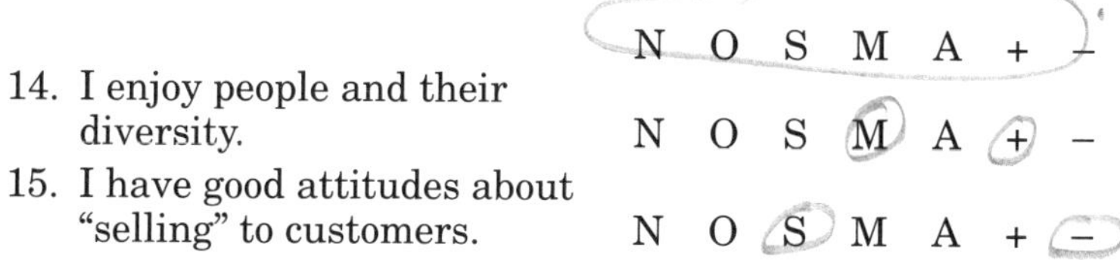

N O S M A + –

14. I enjoy people and their diversity. N O S M A + –
15. I have good attitudes about "selling" to customers. N O S M A + –

For each item for which you circled a minus sign, write a specific and measurable goal for improvement.

RECOGNIZE ORGANIZATIONAL BEHAVIORS THAT CONVEY THE CULTURE

In addition to the individual behaviors described above, a customer also assesses the personality of the entire organization by looking at group behaviors and attitudes. The communication rule that anything can and will communicate still applies for these behaviors, of course. The composite result of group and individual behaviors conveys much about the culture of the organization. If the customer likes your culture, you can be well on your way to building satisfaction and loyalty. Here are some organizational behaviors to consider.

1. The Company's Appearance and Grooming

From the moment we meet people, we begin to size them up. We begin to draw conclusions about them almost immediately. What we decide about their trustworthiness and ability is largely a factor of first impressions, and, as the old saying goes, you only get one chance to make that first impression.

The appearance of an organization's employees is one of the first things seen by customers. Dress standards can set a company apart from the competition and create an E-Plus experience. One way to do this is by looking at what other *successful* companies are doing. You need not be a copycat or wear an outfit you hate, but do consider what other role models do. And then meet or exceed their appearance.

An owner of an auto repair shop tried an experiment. Each of his repair people was paid on commission for the amount of repair work they brought in. He invited the mechanics to volunteer to change their dress and grooming. Several agreed to cut their hair shorter, shave daily, and wear clean uniforms. The outcome was a good example of E-Plus: Those who improved their appearance generated far more repeat business than the others. The customers would ask for the better-dressed mechanics and those who chose to dress and groom themselves in the "old way" found themselves getting less work.

> Employee appearance can have a dramatic effect on business success, especially if it exceeds the expectations of the customers.

Remember, of course, that the key word in dress and grooming is *appropriate.* Salespeople in a surf shop would look foolish in three-piece suits; an undertaker would look ludicrous in a Hawaiian sport shirt and cutoffs. To overcome problems of individual differences that may be inappropriate, some organizations issue uniforms. These may be coveralls, full uniforms, or partial uniforms such as blazers, vests, or work shirts. Some employees like these (they save on the costs of a wardrobe), while some resist the sameness of the uniformed look.

Determine what level of professionalism you want to convey to your customers, then create a look that projects your competence. Your customers notice these things.

2. Check the Appearance of Your Work Area

"A cluttered desk is the sign of a cluttered mind," says the desk plaque. Likewise a cluttered work area conveys a sense of disorganization and low professionalism. Look around you and see what your customer sees. Is merchandise displayed attractively? Is the place clean and tidy? Does the workspace look like an organized, efficient place?

Check, too, for barriers. Often people arrange their work space with a desk, counter, or table between them and the customer. While sometimes this is necessary, often it creates a barrier—both physical and psychological—between the customer and the one serving. Try inviting customers to sit beside your desk with you instead of across from you. Try using a small round table, especially when customers need to read materials you give them. Some auto dealerships have removed all sales office desks and replaced them with small round tables. Now the customer and salesperson sit around the table and work together to make a deal. You don't feel that you are on opposite sides, in "combat" with each other, when the table is round.

> Round tables rather than imposing desks can convey a sense of cooperation rather than opposition between customers and salespeople.

Finally, look for customer comfort. Are your customers invited to sit in a comfortable chair? Does your office or store invite them to relax? Are waiting areas furnished with reading materials, perhaps a TV? Are vending machines available? Is the vending area kept clean?

A small auto body shop I visited surprised me. It had a waiting room that looked like a living room in a nice home, with easy chairs, a TV, coffee table with recent magazines, even fresh flowers.

Recently, auto dealers have begun to emphasize ways to make their car lots and showrooms, many of which are decades old, more attractive and customer-friendly. Some now feature landscaped settings with benches and pathways, different display areas for each auto brand, and interactive systems with screens that show how elements like paint colors and upholstery look together. Take a look at your work areas from the customer's viewpoint.[7]

Service Snapshot

Banks Hang Up on Pesky Customers

What's wrong with this picture?[8] Some loud and clear messages are communicated to customers by these banks.

> As if it weren't bad enough that banks are charging extra fees to serve you at an ATM or even the teller's window, now you may have to pay a fee to call your bank or credit card issuer's customer service telephone line. Or if you phone repeatedly—even to check your balance—you may get an unfriendly letter that scolds you for calling the bank too often.
>
> Some of the biggest financial institutions in the country, including Bank of America and Wells Fargo, are levying punitive fees on frequent callers. Others, including Capital One and Navy Federal Credit Union, are considering similar charges. "Banks have never been famous for customer service, and now some are using customer service departments to generate fees," says Larry Cohn, a senior vice president at PaineWebber.
>
> In the past year Wells Fargo limited customers to three free calls a month; Bank of America imposed a six-call limit. After that, callers are automatically charged 50 cents for each call to an automated information system and $1.50 if they speak to a customer representative.
>
> Capital One isn't charging fees—yet. But it sent letters to about 50,000 customers the bank identified as excessive callers urging them to stop phoning the customer service department so often. The letter reads: "While an occasional inquiry is to be expected, we ask that in the future you limit your phone calls to only those which are truly necessary."
>
> The bank claims that a large number of customers called more than 100 times in a year, and that one person called 700 times. But some customers who received the letter say they called only once or twice—or had to call several times to resolve a single problem. It seems Capital One "cast its net too wide," says Ruth Susswein, executive director of Bankcard Holders of America. Capital One spokeswoman Diana Sun says the bank didn't mean to offend anyone. "We assumed someone who got the letter and had called because of a problem wouldn't think it applied to them," she says. Some of the "problem customers" are taking their business elsewhere.

3. Correspond Regularly

An athletic shoe store and a rental car agency are good examples of this simple idea. A week after purchasing some running shoes, customers receive a handwritten note from the store owner simply thanking them for buying. This is no fancy prose, simply a one- or two-sentence message. It expresses appreciation for their business and invites them to return. An airport car rental agency has employees write thank-you notes to customers when the desk is not busy. The notes are handwritten on the company letterhead and personalized to mention the type of car rented. They thank the customer and invite them to rent again the next time they are in town. The cost of doing this is practically nil since the desk is busy when flights are coming in but then has slow period between arrivals. Why have employees waste time when it's slow when you can have them writing notes?

Don't Let Your Customer Forget You

Another way to not let customers forget you is to send them information about upcoming sales, changes in policies, new promotions, etc. Keep the customer tied in. Likewise, discount coupons or special hours for preferred customers are often appreciated.

> Maintain an open channel of communication with customers via mailouts.

A print shop sends all customers a monthly package of coupons, flyers, and samples, including a printed motivational quote on parchment paper suitable for framing. Additional copies of the quote are available free for the asking. The mailing acts as a reminder of the quality of work the shop can do as well as a promotion.

4. Get the Customer Doing Something

Telling people about your products or services isn't usually enough. Showing them how it works is much better. But to really serve your customers, get them involved and exposed to your corporate culture—get their hands on your products in some way and they'll feel better about you and your company.

Studies of the most successful computer salespeople, for example, show that they encourage customers to sit down at the computer as soon as possible to get them playing with it. They don't dazzle (or confuse) the customer with hi-tech jargon or even information about the machine's capabilities. They get them *doing something.* Likewise, the best auto salespeople invite customers to sit in or test drive the car right away.

Here are other, less obvious ways to get people doing something:

- Personally hand them a shopping cart or basket.

- Ask them to begin filling out paperwork.
- Get them to touch or sample the product.
- Offer a piece of candy or fruit, while they wait.
- Offer a product flyer, information packet, video presentation, or sample to review.

It doesn't matter so much *what* they do, so long as they begin to do *something*.

Get customers doing something with you to expose them to your culture.

Some retailers arrange merchandise so that customers can easily pick it up. Marketing expert Paco Underhill says:

> A trademark of the Gap clothing stores, for example, is that customers can easily touch, stroke, unfold, and otherwise examine at close range anything on the selling floor. A lot of sweaters and shirts are sold thanks to the decision to foster intimate contact between shopper and goods. That merchandising policy dictates the display scheme (wide, flat tabletops, which are easier to shop than racks or shelves). That display scheme in turn determines how and where employees will spend their time; all that touching means that sweaters and shirts constantly need to be refolded and straightened and neatened. That translates into the need for lots of clerks roaming the floor rather than standing behind the counter ringing up sales. Which is a big expense, but for Gap and others, it's a sound investment—the cost of doing business.[9]

This is yet another way of E-Plussing customers with organizational personality.

5. Use Hoopla and Fun

People enjoy working in an organization where they have fun. Successful companies have regular rituals—whether it be Friday afternoon popcorn, birthday parties, or employee-of-the-month celebrations—that everyone gets involved in. Excellent organizations are fun places to work; they create rituals of their own.

As a manager at a utility company, I initiated frequent sales contests, complete with skits and prizes. Each time a particular product was sold, the service representative could pop a balloon and find a prize inside it, ranging from a $10 bill to a coupon good for a piece of pie in the company cafeteria. Employees loved it and got involved.

Other ideas are:

- Employee (or hero) of the week or month recognition.
- Awards luncheons (include some tongue-in-cheek "awards").
- A day off with pay.
- Casual dress days.

- Halloween costume day.
- Family picnics.

Don't fall into the trap of thinking these things are hokey. Employees at all levels enjoy celebrations and hoopla, and their effects spread to the customer.

6. Reward the Right Actions

Fairly often, organizations inadvertently reward one behavior while hoping for something else. In such cases the company *hopes* something happens but actually rewards a counterbehavior. For example, a company rewards individuals and departments for never receiving complaints. The hope is that, by receiving no complaints, it can assume that everyone is doing a good job. The reality, however, may well be that complaints are being suppressed. Customers have no effective way to voice complaints. Instead, they just quit doing business with the company.

As we discussed earlier, it's not bad news to receive a complaint; it *is* bad news to suppress a complaint. Some percentage of customers are always less than satisfied, and ignoring them does no good. Quite the contrary, you must draw out those customer concerns so that they can be addressed and corrected. As someone once said, "Even the ostrich leaves one end exposed."

> Companies sometimes reward "A" while hoping for "B."

Here are some other examples of possible reward conflicts whereby the wrong behaviors may be rewarded and the right behaviors ignored:

- *Rewarding employees for fast transaction handling when customers may be left uninformed or resent being rushed along.* For example, a restaurant that encourages employees to get the customer fed and out quickly may create unhappy customers who prefer to eat more slowly. Or if the electronic equipment buyer does not understand how to work the features of the VCR before leaving the dealership, he or she might feel unhappy with the purchase.
- *Encouraging salespeople to "cooperate with each other to best meet the customer needs" while paying a straight commission.* For example, salespeople practically trip over each other to approach new customers before the other guy gets to them.
- *Encouraging employees to send thank-you notes to customers but never allowing on-the-job time to do so.* This creates the impression that it really isn't that important.
- *Constantly stressing the need to reduce the amount of return merchandise by docking the pay of clerks who accept too many returns.* As a result, customers encounter reluctance to take back unsatisfactory products.

- *Paying people by the hour instead of by the task accomplished.* Hourly wages are simpler to administer but they basically pay people for using up time!

Check your organization. Are you really rewarding the right behaviors?

The reward system within an organization needs to be tilted to the advantage of the employee who provides excellent service. Any rewards should be given in direct relationship to the employee's contribution to customer service, consistent with the theme you've selected.

Rewards take many forms, some obvious, some more subtle:

- Salary and cash bonuses
- Prizes and awards
- Promotions and job enrichment
- Preferred work locations, better offices, larger desks
- Work scheduling flexibility
- Pins, badges, uniforms
- Reserved parking space
- "Employee of the week (or month)" recognition
- Compliments, spoken or in writing
- Surprise recognition parties or celebrations
- Lunches or banquets
- Newsletter writeups

Management is limited only by its imagination when it comes to rewarding employees. But the most important point is that *managers reward the right actions and results.*

7. Stay Close after the Sale

Customers hate a love-'em-and-leave-'em relationship. Yet many companies offer just that. Once the sale is made, the customer goes back to feeling like a stranger. *Look for opportunities to contact the customer after the sale.* Establish ongoing friendships and customers will keep coming back.

Here are some ideas for contacting customers after the sale:

- Mail thank-you notes.
- Call to be sure the product or service met their needs.
- Send out new product information.
- Send clippings of interest or newsworthy information that may reassure customers of their good purchasing decisions.
- Send birthday and holiday cards.
- Invite customers to participate in a focus group.
- Call to thank them for referrals.

Another Look

The Sour Smell of Poor Customer Service[10]

Dr. Richards, president of a Toronto-based marketing consultancy and a frequent speaker on customer service, had this to say:

> The drive to "listen to the customer" is the new mantra for American business, and customer service is the latest growth industry for consultants. Boardrooms are reverberating with the sound of CEOs preaching the gospel of "getting close to our customer." However, there is a remarkable chasm between these head-office professions of commitment to the customer and the actual behavior toward those self-same customers down the line.
>
> This fall in the course of conducting 22 marketing workshops across the U.S., our firm found that gap to be painfully evident.
>
> We used a variety of hotels for these workshops, including three from a chain that has become synonymous with customer service (I'll refrain from naming the chain because I have consulted with one of its chief competitors).
>
> We were asked by all three to fill out slightly different credit applications. The credit department in each case insisted that a copy of its sister hotel's form was insufficient and that only its own would do; only under duress did it accept a copy of the credit application from another member of the chain (which incidentally, contained all the information it asked for, simply in a different format).
>
> In arranging for people to register attendees at these workshops, we dealt with one of the national chains of temporary staff, Office Overload. We were pleased to find that we could deal with one individual who would arrange all the bookings for us. But billing was another matter. No matter how hard we tried, we could not get consolidated billing. As a result, we received 22 different bills from 22 different locations—and had to write 22 checks for $200 or less.
>
> Out for dinner with a client after one of the workshops, we walked into the local outpost of a well-known chain of midpriced Italian restaurants, Olive Garden. At our request for a nonsmoking table, we got the response that every abstainer will recognize: "It will take about 20 minutes for a table in nonsmoking, but there's a table right at the edge of the smoking section that I can let you have right away."
>
> I countered with what seemed like a perfectly reasonable proposition. "Seat us in smoking for now and move us into nonsmoking when that opens up."
>
> The reply, "I'm sorry, sir, I can't do that," provoked an unsympathetic response. "Do you mean to tell me that with modern technology we can send a man to the moon and bring him back, but you can't start us at one table and then move us to another?"
>
> We did ultimately get our way—but only grudgingly and with the clear sense that we were being unreasonable in the extreme.
>
> This is by no means an exhaustive list. Any traveler can regale you with tales of unresponsive, uncaring service. Which leads to the simple question: What's going on here? How is that these paragons of customer commitment at the head office ignore, insult and otherwise frustrate customers in their actual dealings?

The sources of this problem are more numerous than can be dealt with here—ranging from front-line employees and middle management entrenched in old, familiar patterns or a simple failure to communicate on the part of senior management.

There is, however, another factor at work here—what, for lack of a better description, I call the "Takla syndrome." Early in my career, business took me to a pulp and paper mill in Takla, a small community in the interior of British Columbia.

As we approached, I was hit by a distinct and overwhelming odor, which I subsequently discovered was sulfur. As discreetly as I could, I asked my client, a longtime resident, how people put up with the smell. His response: "Smell? What smell?"

He was quite serious. After awhile, people who lived in Takla simply became inured to the smell—they didn't notice it anymore. In fact, for them, it didn't exist.

And that, I believe, is what's happening when we encounter those nonresponsive employees. Often, they've lived with the smell of poor customer service for so long that they don't notice it anymore.

If you want to effect change, the first thing you have to do is get your people to understand the frustrations your customers face, to get them to walk through the buying experience from the customer's point of view.

There are many methods that will help sensitize front-line staff. One of the simplest and most effective is to videotape some customers actually talking about what they find frustrating in dealing with your company. It's remarkable how quickly you see lights go on when those tapes get played back.

How you sensitize your employees doesn't really matter. What is important is that you understand the barrier represented by the Takla syndrome. Unless you deal with this problem, all your talk about listening to the customer will just frustrate those of your clients foolish enough to believe you actually mean it.

Probes

1. What are some of the specific behaviors cited in this reading that caused the customer's dissatisfaction?
2. To what extent do the customer turnoffs arise from value, systems, and people?
3. What actions would you, as a manager, take to remedy the customer problems described in this article?

A FINAL THOUGHT

Individual and organizational behaviors are conveyed to customers via little things. Often people are unaware of how they are coming across and are therefore at a distinct disadvantage. Broadening our awareness of how other people read our verbal and nonverbal messages is a useful step in improving customer service.

Likewise, just as individuals project their behaviors to customers, so do organizations. The company's collective behavior patterns constitute its culture and may be perceived as favorable or unfavorable by customers (internal and external). The ways managers and leaders interact with subordinates and associates have considerable impact on the way all people behave toward customers.

Summary of Key Ideas

- Behavior is what people do. It is conveyed via verbal or nonverbal communication.
- Individual actions as well as organizational behaviors convey messages to customers that may have a positive or negative effect on their perception of service received.
- Any behaviors (or lack of behaviors) can communicate; the receiver of the message (e.g., the customer) determines what the message means.
- Exceeding expectations in the area of personality (as discussed in our VISPAC acronym in Chapter 4) depends on both individual actions and the organization's behaviors or culture.
- Individual behaviors that impact customer service include greeting customers, breaking the ice by initiating conversation, complimenting, calling people by name, establishing and maintaining eye contact, asking for feedback, listening skillfully, saying please and thank you, reassuring customer buying decisions, smiling, using good telephone techniques, being sensitive to timing, appropriate touching behaviors, enjoying people, and being positive about selling.
- Organizational behaviors that tell the customer about your culture include the appearance and grooming of employees, the appearance of work areas, the frequency and quality of correspondence with customers, the propensity to get customers doing something relevant to the buying decision, use of hoopla and fun to celebrate company successes, reward systems that motivate appropriate employee behaviors, and staying close to the customer after the sale.

Key Terms and Concepts

Appropriate touching
Behavior
Getting the customer committed
Hoopla and fun
Icebreakers
Organization culture
Personality
Reward the right actions
The three "I's" of eye communication: intimacy, intimidation, involvement
Verbal discipline

Self-Test Questions

1. What constitutes behavior? How is it conveyed?
2. How can an organization's culture impact customer service?
3. What are some of the behaviors that project individual personality?
4. What are icebreakers? How can they best be used? Give a few examples.
5. What are sources of compliments you can use for your internal and external customers?
6. What are the three I's of eye communication?
7. What are some tips you can use to be a better listener?
8. How can you use physical touch as a way to exceed the customer's expectations? Give an example.
9. What are some factors that project a company's culture? List several examples.
10. Why is it important for companies to reward the right actions of their employees?

Application Activity: Does Behavior Influence Customer Loyalty?

This chapter implies a strong relationship between behaviors (of individuals and organizations) and the likelihood of customer loyalty. Let's test that idea.

On pages 118–119 are two simple data-gathering forms. The first lists the behaviors discussed in the chapter and invites customers to rate them. The second form asks three simple questions about customer loyalty. We call this the Customer Loyalty Index (CLI).

Your task is to gather input by interviewing ten or more customers of a business or organization. Use the same business for all responses. Follow the interview guide word for word. Have each respondent answer "yes," "no," or "unsure or not applicable."

NOTES

[1]D. Berry, "Booth Won't Take Toll, but Bad Attitude Will," Knight-Ridder Newspapers, April 7, 1991. Reprinted with permission.

[2]Many of the ideas in this section are adapted from P. Timm, *50 Powerful Ideas You Can Use to Keep Your Customers,* 2nd ed. (Hawthorne, NJ: Career Press, 1995). Copyright Paul R. Timm.

[3]Cited in the "Yamaha Merchandising Training," Yamaha Corp. Also found in Sam Geist, *Why Should Someone Do Business with You Rather Than Someone Else?* (ISBN 1-896984-00-2), p. 98.

Interview Guide

Part I. Behavior Questionnaire

When you last did business with ______________________, did the employees there:

1.	Greet you promptly?	Yes	No	? or NA
2.	Use opening comments to help you feel at ease?	Yes	No	? or NA
3.	Compliment you in any way?	Yes	No	? or NA
4.	Call you by your name?	Yes	No	? or NA
5.	Make and maintain eye contact with you?	Yes	No	? or NA
6.	Ask for feedback from you in any way?	Yes	No	? or NA
7.	Listen carefully to your needs or wants?	Yes	No	? or NA
8.	Say "please" and "thank you"?	Yes	No	? or NA
9.	Reassure your decisions to do business with them?	Yes	No	? or NA
10.	Smile freely and often?	Yes	No	? or NA
11.	Use good telephone techniques?	Yes	No	? or NA
12.	Act sensitive to timing and follow up with you?	Yes	No	? or NA
13.	Appropriately touch you (shake hand, pat you on the back, etc.)?	Yes	No	? or NA
14.	Seem to enjoy people and their diversity?	Yes	No	? or NA
15.	Seem to have good attitudes about selling?	Yes	No	? or NA
16.	Keep the workplace clean and attractive?	Yes	No	? or NA
17.	Dress and groom themselves appropriately?	Yes	No	? or NA
18.	Seem to enjoy working for this company?	Yes	No	? or NA

Part II. Customer Loyalty Index

1. Overall, how satisfied were you with [name of company or organization]?

Extremely unsatisfied	Unsatisfied	Neutral	Satisfied	Extremely satisfied

2. How likely would you be to recommend [name of company or organization] to a friend or associate?

   Very unlikely Not likely Maybe Very likely Certain

3. How likely are you to do business with [name of company or organization] again?

   Very unlikely Not likely Maybe Very likely Certain

Scoring: For Part I of the interview, the behaviors, score one point for each "yes" response. Total possible = 18.

For Part II the CLI, score each item on a five-point scale from left to right (e.g., the most negative response is a 1, the most positive a 5, and those in between 2, 3, or 4).

After you have tallied scores for your entire sample (minimum of 10), write a brief analysis of the results. Comment especially on the behaviors that most seem to relate to customer loyalty, as customers see them.

[4]B. Decker, *The Art of Communication* (Menlo Park, CA: Crisp Publications, Inc., 1988), p. 17.

[5]An excellent 30-minute videotape training program featuring the author is *Winning Telephone Techniques,* produced by JWA Video in Chicago. For information, call 312-829-5100.

[6]These ideas are found in E. N. Chapman, *The Fifty Minute Sales Training Program* (Menlo Park, CA: Crisp Publications, Inc., 1992).

[7]"A Picnic in a Car Lot?" *Wall Street Journal,* October 13, 1994, p. A-1.

[8]Excerpted from "Banks Hang Up on Pesky Customers," *Kiplinger's Personal Finance Magazine,* August 1996, pp. 84–85. Reprinted with permission of The Kiplinger Washington Editors, Inc.

[9]Paco Underhill, "What Shoppers Want," *Inc.,* July 1999, p. 76.

[10]D. Richards, "Sour Smell of Poor Customer Service," *Wall Street Journal,* December 28, 1992, p. A–10. Reprinted with permission.

Foundation Skill

6

Get Others to Give Great Service

Roles of the Supervisor, Manager, or Leader

If you want a good indication of the quality of your people management, ask your customers how they are being treated by your employees.

—Ken Blanchard

WHAT YOU'LL LEARN IN THIS CHAPTER

- The central thread running through all management functions is communication, and organizations suffer when communication is ineffective.
- You can lead people in articulating an effective customer service credo or theme.
- You can set objectives and develop an effective customer satisfaction strategy.
- Potentially disquieting (yet penetrating) questions can readily point to customer service problems.
- You can manage the service process with questions.

- There are ways to instruct and motivate employees to provide quality customer service.
- Seven critical tasks that can initiate and sustain an E-Plus customer loyalty strategy.

The Way It Is

The Role of Managers and Leaders in Providing Customer Service

A recent national news magazine carried a letter from a reader who was responding to a story critical of the poor service given by a large retailer. This retailer had seen its profits fall dramatically. The reader said:

> I found [the story] extremely timely and on the mark. Having spent the past 20 years in sales and marketing, 10 of them in discount and upscale retail management, I still can't decide if the [Company's] posture has been one of "you snooze, you lose" or simple corporate arrogance. Perhaps [the company] may just now be waking up to the fact that you can no longer abuse your customers and get away with it. Your article spoke of [an] example where only four checkout lanes out of 12 were open. We also see four checkout lanes open, with a dozen customers in each lane, the manager on duty and head cashier standing with arms crossed at the service desk surveying the chaos. On one trip, when I asked the manager why he didn't either open a register himself or bag items for the checkers, he responded that it wasn't his job.
>
> My heart goes out for the well-being of the quality folks who work at the stores. Regardless of their efforts, they can only raise the level of quality up to that point "allowed" by the corporate structure and support mechanisms.[1]

Is this reader fair in placing the blame for poor service on management? This chapter considers that question as we examine the roles of managers and leaders in providing customer service.

DO THE WORK OF MANAGEMENT

As a reader of this book, you are very likely preparing for or currently in a management position in an organization. By "management position" I am referring to any situation in which a person supervises, coordinates, or leads the efforts of other people. The manager's job calls for an ability to get others to do the right things in addition to doing the right things oneself. The ability to multiply one's efforts explains why managers are typically paid more and why skilled managers are always in demand. Their impact on an organization can be dramatic. Employees tend to live up—or down—to their manager's expectations of them.

The Functions of Management

The manager's job consists of four key functions: planning, organizing, coordinating, and controlling. Let's look at each function as it relates to customer service.

1. *Planning* is a thinking process, a sort of internal communication within one's mind. The manager looks ahead to what must be done to maintain and improve performance, to solve problems, and to develop employee competence. To plan, a manager sets objectives in each area that is to be pursued this week, this month, this year. Having set these objectives, the manager then thinks through such questions as:
   - What has to be done to reach these objectives?
   - How will these activities be carried out?
   - Who will do them?
   - When will these activities take place?
   - Where will this work be done?
   - What resources will be needed?

   Done well, such planning requires asking questions of customers, both internal and external, and determining what to do in the future based on the input received.

> Effective planning involves gathering information and projecting future outcomes.

2. *Organizing* involves arranging the work sequence and assigning areas of responsibility and authority. Having decided the objectives and activities of the work unit, the manager must:
   - Assign these responsibilities to employees.
   - Give employees the supporting authority to fulfill their responsibilities.

   Done well, this management work reduces potential systems turnoffs caused by ineffective staffing, poor training, inefficient work layout, etc. Remember that "systems" involve anything having to do with the deliv-

> The management responsibility to reduce systems turnoffs often involves organizing.

ery of products or services to the customer. (Review Chapter 1, if necessary, to refresh your memory about customer turnoffs.) Constantly organizing and improving systems is a major leadership responsibility.

3. *Coordinating* is often summed up in the term *leading*. Managers lead by enabling the organization to achieve its objectives. To do this, they:
   - Show (by example) what subordinates should do.
   - Generate the energy (motivation) that subordinates must feel.
   - Provide the needed resources to accomplish the tasks.

   What leaders do in an organization sets the tone for motivation throughout. *Motivation* can be simply defined as "providing motives for action." Leaders provide motives or reasons why people should act in particular ways.

4. *Controlling* is the function of ensuring that employees are working toward the selected objectives. It involves comparing actual results to expected or planned-for results so as to identify any deviation from plan. Typically, any deviation calls for using different motivation attempts, adjusting activities so as to close the gap, or changing the objectives to make them more realistic.

> Controlling is a process of following up to be certain that planned-for actions are, in fact, being carried out. Managers inspect what they expect.

The Common Thread in Management Functions

Each of these management functions involves *people*. Herein lies the universal characteristic of the manager's job: Only when managers *accomplish work with and through other people* are they doing the job correctly.

> The essence of the manager's job is to accomplish work with and through other people.

RECOGNIZE THAT GOOD MANAGEMENT REQUIRES GOOD COMMUNICATION

To ensure smooth functioning of any organization, managers must maintain an ongoing flow of appropriate communication. Communication is crucial to all management functions. *Three types of poor communication can damage organizational results.* Organizations fail to maximize their effectiveness and create customer service problems when:

1. *Too little communication* takes place.
2. *Too much communication* is attempted.
3. *Ineffective communication* is widespread.

Let's consider each of these conditions.

Too Little Communication

Crumbling relationships and dysfunctional families often result from too little communication. Countless marriages fail primarily because couples withhold expressions of appreciation, concern, or ideas. People who cannot express their feelings to each other in marriage seldom succeed in a family organization.

Likewise, businesses in which customers are not asked about their needs, employees have insufficient product knowledge, or employees don't know which behaviors are appropriate run a huge risk of internal confusion and poor service success. Good organizations keep their people well trained and fully informed. Great organizations constantly solicit information from stakeholders (all people who share an interest in the company's success) and act on it.

> Keeping people informed and getting a constant flow of information from stakeholders are characteristics of strong organizations.

Too Much Communication

Going to the opposite extreme can be a problem too. People who find themselves bombarded with too much information, much of it irrelevant, may collapse under the load. This is the organizational equivalent of the old quip, "I asked him what time it was and he told me how to build a watch." Smart companies keep people informed of things they need to know or may want to know, but don't bombard them with trivia.

> Communication overload can cripple an organization and damage employee productivity.

Widespread Ineffective Communication

Widespread ineffective communication also results in organizational failure, for several reasons. Among the most common are unclear direction or coordination, inadequate processing of important data, and missed organizational opportunities. Some examples of ineffective communication are the overuse of poorly planned meetings, failure to publicize accomplishments, poor telephone techniques, or ineffective writing.

RECOGNIZE THAT CUSTOMERS LIKE ORGANIZATIONS THAT COMMUNICATE WELL

I've asked thousands of people at training sessions to think about places they regularly do business with and then asked for specific reasons why they kept going back. In every group I get responses like these:

- The waitresses (or proprietors or clerks) are really friendly. They call me by name and seem genuinely interested in me.
- Old Phil at the gas station waves when I drive by.
- Mike the butcher listens to me when I ask for a special cut of meat.
- Sarah's so friendly—she's always willing to help.
- Doc Peterson's nurses are really nice. They seem to take a real interest in the kids.

> The greatest cause of lost customers: They feel badly treated.

The words are different, but the theme is almost always the same: The organization, through its people, *communicates* a sense of caring. Conversely, studies conducted by the Forum Corporation interviewed customers lost in business-to-business relationships (one business buying from another). The research concluded that 69 percent of business customers who stopped buying were lost not because of product quality or cost, but because they felt badly treated.[2] Good communication goes a long way to reduce such feelings.

> A lack of caring is clearly communicated, even if not in words.

When we asked people what organizations they "hate to do business with," respondents cited organizations whose people convey a sense that:

"You [the customer] are an intrusion."

"We really don't care whether you are satisfied or not."

"I hate my job and it's partly your fault."

"I can't be bothered with you now."

Employees don't say these things out loud, of course, but they do convey these impressions.

An obvious and significant challenge for managers is to be sensitive to the ways their employees communicate to the world around them—especially customers.

REMEMBER THAT THE CUSTOMER DETERMINES COMMUNICATION SUCCESS

Another point about the nature of communication is important: *We really can't control communication.* We can, and must, seek to influence it, but ultimately the customer determines the meaning of any messages we send. This inconvenient reality is frustrating to people who naively think they can control 100 percent of their communication outcomes. It's not that simple.

> Although we cannot ultimately control communication, we can learn effective ways to influence it.

Communicating with another person is not a science; it is an art. No magic checklist of precise and exacting procedures exists. Specific, sound principles and themes can be learned, but there are thousands of variations on these themes.

Developing the art of communication often means letting go of old assumptions and getting out of the comfortable rut of communicating as usual. Improvement has little to do with talking louder, more emphatically, or more earnestly. It may have little to do with increasing the amount of information we give others. It has little to do with making the message sound better and better to us. It has everything to do with *developing more understanding.* This means looking at the world through the eyes of others, walking the proverbial mile in another's moccasins. Most of us are hesitant to do this, but it is exactly this kind of thinking that leads to meaningful improvement in communication.

EMPLOY SPECIFIC MANAGEMENT FUNCTIONS FOR CUSTOMER SERVICE

Let's take a closer look at key management functions as they apply to customer service. Several specific actions we can take to work with and through other people can have a dramatic impact on customer satisfaction and loyalty.

Articulate a Service Theme

The planning function includes management efforts to articulate a vision, forecasting where the organization would like to go. One idea found useful for many organizations is to develop a service theme, credo, or mission statement.

As I consult with organizations, I typically ask if they have a customer service theme or credo. Fairly often I get answers something like, "Oh, yes, we have 13 points for excellent customer service."

I'd reply, "Oh, really? What's point 11?" and the manager would say, "Well, I don't know exactly." Then I'd ask, "Well, how about point six? Which one's that?" And again the typical answer is, "I'm not sure, I actually haven't memorized all these things, but every employee has a copy and we post our mission statement throughout the company."

Unfortunately, if the credo is too complex, it doesn't do much good. To articulate a theme means to come up with a succinct, clear statement of what the organization is about and how it can be seen as unique in the eyes of the customer.

Let's go through that one more time. An effective service theme must be:

- succinct,
- clear, and
- descriptive of uniqueness.

Someone once said that one criteria for a good mission statement or theme is that, "You could repeat it at gunpoint!"[3]

You want it succinct and clear so that every employee can remember and "buy into" it as a guiding statement that shapes their actions and helps them make decisions. Let's look at a couple of examples.

Federal Express, the package delivery service, has a simple, clear theme. They express it in three words: "Absolutely, positively, overnight." They get the packages there absolutely, positively, overnight, and they're 99.8 percent successful at doing that. The direct marketing clothier, Lands' End, has a simple motto or credo that has just two words: "Guaranteed. Period." Both of these themes communicate the company's highest customer service priority.

A *Harvard Business Review*[4] article told of a Seattle restaurant staff who wrestled with this idea of a simple, clear theme. After carefully looking at the company through the eyes of their customer—just what does our restaurant guest want from us?—they came up with this theme: "Your enjoyment guaranteed. Always." That is exactly what they offer their guests—enjoyment.

A neat thing about this simple theme was that people could buy into it, and in fact they made it into an acronym: YEGA. While YEGA may not mean anything to most of us, it became a catchword for their organization. They developed YEGA promotions, YEGA bucks, and YEGA pins and hats to get their employees involved in the spirit. It was fun, it was interesting, and it reminded the employees constantly of that simple, four-word theme: "Your enjoyment guaranteed. Always."

Here is what managers can do to articulate a good theme:

- *Commit* to work on the process of identifying a theme that is *succinct, clear, and descriptive* of your uniqueness.

- *Gather ideas from your customers (internal and external).* Ask them, "What five things do you want as customers in doing business with us?" Ask them to respond quickly, off the tops of their heads, and look at the language they use.
- Similarly, gather your own people and ask, *"If you were our customer, what five things would you like to get from a company like ours?"* Ask people to respond quickly. Jot down the language and then collect all the words. Front-line people know the customers best and can give you great ideas. Never overlook the ideas of this group of experts.

> Listen for key words from customers and customer-contact employees as you develop a theme.

As you gather perceptions from customers and employees, you'll notice that some terms come up over and over again. These typically are the kinds of words that reassure your customer. These are good words to put into your customer service theme.

As you draft a theme for your organization, remember:

- Use the participation and input from customers and employees. The customers can best tell you what they're looking for in an organization like yours, and the employees' participation ensures that they will accept and live by the intention of the theme.
- Write several rough drafts of the theme; don't be too quick to come up with the finished version. Phrase the final version in ten or fewer words.
- If possible, try to make the theme into an acronym, so the first letters of each word form a word in themselves, as in the YEGA example given earlier.

When you've identified a statement of uniqueness, ask yourself the question, Would everyone in the organization choose roughly the same words you chose to describe this distinctiveness? A simple way to verify this is to stop some of your employees and ask them to describe the organization's theme. Especially invite an employee who's been with the organization for ten days or less to identify the theme.

What good does it do just to be able to repeat such a phrase? The answer is that it's a start. Repeating some words may seem meaningless at first, but most organizations fall far short even of that level of agreement. Focusing your people on a common theme can be well worth the effort.

One final note: A theme is not necessarily forever. As an organization changes directions, as markets or economic conditions change, a theme may be modified. Some organizations may want to use a theme statement for a limited period of time, much the way advertisers use a slogan for only a few years. Modifying the theme should not, however, be done without careful thought. Consistency of direction is in itself valuable.

Important: If you have employees participate in clarifying a theme, they feel more committed to it. Participation leads to buy-in. This has been shown time and again since the earliest studies in human relations.

Be sure to involve employees and customers in developing a service theme.

Set Objectives and Develop a Service Strategy

The next management planning function involves determining desired service end results and deciding how and when to achieve service goals. Goal setting has long been recognized as a powerful tool for focusing effort. Be sure that targeted improvements are measurable and reasonable. Changes in organizational behaviors and results take time. Don't rush the process. Goal setting helps establish the priorities, sequence, and timing of strategy steps. You can't fix everything at once; so look for the kinds of results that can give you the most impact relative to the effort involved. Pick the low-hanging fruit first. Handling the obvious shortcomings can motivate the troops to tackle the more difficult problems later.

Managers typically need to budget for improvements. Many changes, especially those that attack systems or value turnoffs, require the expenditure of money or other resources. Once better methods are developed, establish them as policy—as standing decisions on how the organization is to work.

Organize People and Delineate Authority

The organizing function of management involves such actions as clarifying the organizational structure, assigning certain responsibilities, and giving authority to organization members. People at all levels need to know the scope and range of their jobs. Employees need to understand what they can or cannot do for customers.

Among companies giving legendary service, people at all levels are given a lot of latitude. Nordstrom employees know they can do almost anything to meet a customer's needs. They have been known to send clothing to customers using overnight delivery (regardless of the additional cost) and to give customers an add-on to compensate for any disappointment. Ritz-Carlton hotel employees are encouraged to take personal "ownership" for any problem a guest may have. If a guest's need comes to their attention, they drop what they are doing and solve the problem or meet the guest's need. Bellhops have been known to rush out of the hotel to buy a foreign newspaper for a guest who was disappointed that the publication wasn't available in the hotel's gift shop. No questions are asked; managers have given bellhops the authority to do whatever it takes. This may be one reason that Ritz-Carlton won the prestigious Baldridge Award for corporate excellence.

Staff with Quality Employees

Managers are responsible for recruiting qualified people for each employee position, orienting new people to the company's service expectations, and providing training so that people become proficient through instruction and practice.

Some successful managers recruit by stealing good employees from other companies. (That's stated a bit too strongly, but the principle works.) As managers come across people with great attitudes and excellent customer service skills, they might try to hire them away or at least recommend them to company recruiters.

One owner of a chain of fast-food restaurants solved his problem of getting quality people in a high-turnover industry by giving his business card to employees of other companies who wait on him. He'd say something like, "Thank you for your great service. You did a nice job. If you are ever interested in changing jobs, I'd appreciate it if you'd call me personally. I'm sure I could find a place for you in my organization."

An ongoing process should be to keep a file of people you'd like to have working for you and when an opening occurs, contact them. Don't worry if they are working in a totally different type of business. The specifics of your organization can be taught. Great attitudes cannot.

Managers need to be sure that, once hired, people have ample opportunity to develop their knowledge, attitudes, and skills. The best jobs are those that allow people to grow.

Direct the Company's Efforts

Managers fulfill their directing functions by delegating. This means assigning responsibility and accountability for service results to the people they manage. They also need to motivate by persuading and inspiring people to take desired action. Other directing functions include coordinating desired efforts in the most efficient combination, managing differences, resolving conflicts, and stimulating creativity and innovation in achieving service goals.

Control the Organization

Managers need to determining what critical service data are needed to track important results. They can then measure key results and compare them with the goals or standards. Control also involves taking corrective action by coaching people to help them attain standards or by adjusting the plan as needed. Finally, providing rewards is a crucial part of controlling and motivating.

Managers have a lot to do, as you can see.

ASK SOME POTENTIALLY DISQUIETING QUESTIONS

A starting point for determining how well an organization is doing with customer service may be to answer questions like the ones below. A positive response to one or more of these may not be devastating, but if you answer yes to most of them, your organization is likely to face an uphill battle to substantially improve customer service.

Self-Analysis

Some Potentially Disquieting Questions

Does your company, organization, or department:

1. Talk about customer service but pay front-line people a low, flat wage?
2. Offer little or no training in the fundamentals of customer service for customer-contact people?
3. Offer no special incentives for taking care of the customer?
4. Punish or reprimand employees' poor customer service but take good service for granted?
5. Place greater emphasis on winning new customers than on retaining ones it already has?
6. Offer no awards or recognition for non-customer-contact people's efforts to serve customers?
7. Hold "be nice to the customer" programs or campaigns that last for a few weeks or months but are soon forgotten?
8. Have top managers who rarely if ever devote time to listening to customers and helping them solve problems?
9. Make no effort to measure service quality as perceived by customers?
10. Make no attempt to ensure that managers at all levels are accountable for and rewarded on the basis of service?

Most managers would have to answer "yes" to several of these questions. That, in itself, is not an indicator of poor service policies, but it could point to potential problem areas. Asking lots of penetrating questions can be a valuable management activity.

MANAGE WITH QUESTIONS

Author Bill Maynard[5] agrees that the art of management often involves asking lots of questions. He recommends that, as managers interact with people throughout the organization as well as with customers, they ask questions like these:

What made you mad today?
What took too long?
What caused complaints today?
What was misunderstood today?
What costs too much?
What was too complicated?
What was just plain silly?
What job involved too many people?
What job involved too many actions?
What was wasted?

An effective manager would be wise to commit these questions to memory and ask them often. Then, of course, it is crucial that they act on the answers people give, whenever possible.

Self-Analysis

Understand Your Feedback Receptiveness Attitude

Think back to the last time you received criticism from someone else. Recall a specific event or situation. Describe it in a few sentences. Now mentally review the situation. To what degree did you:

1. Hold back on defending or explaining yourself until the full criticism was fully expressed?
2. Work to understand the criticizer's point of view as best you could?
3. Ask for elaboration or clarification without being overly defensive?
4. Express an honest reaction?
5. Thank the person for the feedback?

For most people, *giving* criticism (even in a constructive way) is risky. When people first offer such feedback, they watch closely to gauge the receiver's responses. The reaction they receive usually determines whether they offer feedback again. This means that *you* have the opportunity to avoid turning off future feedback that could be valuable to you.

Overall, how would you rate your attitude when you are given feedback? What might you change, if anything?

SPEND TIME TO INSTRUCT AND MOTIVATE EMPLOYEES

"Management by walking around" has, in recent years, been seen as an increasingly important function of the manager. The practice increases opportunities for giving recognition and gaining insights from the people "on the firing line." The payoff goes beyond mere pleasant interpersonal relations; it shows up in better motivation and clearer communication among organization members.

Managers can have a profound effect on their employees by simply thanking or complimenting them. It sounds simplistic, but the fact remains that, as Robert Townsend said in *Up the Organization,* "Thanks [are] a really neglected form of compensation."[6]

Express Approval to Create Worker Motivation

Management consultants recommend systematic approaches to expressing verbal approval that have demonstrated remarkable results. What is a *systematic* approach to expressing verbal approval? The most common one is based in a psychological approach called *behavior modification.*

First, managers typically implement such a systematic program by holding a series of meetings in which managers and employees discuss mutual needs and problems as well as potential solutions. Key data are "benchmarked" to measure a starting point. These diagnostic sessions provide a base for determining job performance standards and how they will be met. The meetings also identify rewards that managers may use to "modify" the employees' behavior.

The second step is to arrange for worker performance to be observed with reliable follow-up.

The third step is to give feedback often, immediately letting employees know how their current level of performance compares with the level desired. For example, in one early attempt, an airline company with five telephone reservation offices employing about 1,800 people kept track of the percentage of calls in which callers make flight reservations. Then they fed back the results daily to each employee. At the same time, supervisors were instructed to praise employees for asking callers for their reservations. Within a few months, the ratio of sales to calls soared from one in four to one in two.[7] It was as simple as counting how often employees asked for the customer's business.

> The objective of such a program is to reward systematically—to tie the reward to specific performance.

Use the Psychology of Change

At the heart of any performance improvement is the premise that *future behavior is influenced by the outcomes of past behavior.* If the outcome immediately following an act is in some way rewarding, people are likely to repeat the behavior. If the response is punishing, people are likely not to do it again. Managers, then, can provide three types of communicated responses to employee behaviors. The normal effects of each response on employee behavior are as follows:

• Positive reinforcement . . .	➧ encourages employee to repeat the behavior.
• Negative reinforcement . . .	➧ encourages employee to avoid the behavior in the future.
• No observable response at all . . .	➧ usually causes the employee to extinguish the behavior (no incentive for continuing is given).

Some people question just how far we can go with verbal approval as a motivator. Theoretically, it should work indefinitely as long as appropriate *schedules of reinforcement* are used. The two main reinforcement schedules are *continuous* and *intermittent.* Continuous reinforcement means individuals receive reinforcement (a compliment or supportive statement) every time they engage in the desired behavior. This approach is useful when people are being taught a new behavior and need to be shored up to develop confidence in this new ability. People learn very quickly, at least initially, under continuous reinforcement.

Continuous reinforcement gets quick performance results initially.

You can readily see the results of continuous reinforcement when teaching a small child how to do something like catching a ball. If, each time the ball is caught, you praise the child, the child develops this skill very quickly. The principle generally holds for employees working on unfamiliar tasks.

Yet the use of continuous reinforcement poses at least three problems:

1. It takes too much time, and it therefore costs a great deal in terms of supervisory effort. It is just not feasible to always be complimenting each job done. You might as well do the job yourself!
2. It can diminish in effectiveness because of "inflation." Verbal approval can be cheapened by overuse.
3. Once continuous reinforcement is expected, it is tough to wean people away from it without certain risks. If we suddenly drop continuous reinforcement—that is, we no longer express verbal approval for each good behavior—the message to our worker may be that the behavior is no longer appropriate and should be stopped. In short, we may extinguish the desired behavior.

Random, intermittent reinforcement can lead to longer-term motivation.

The drawbacks to continuous reinforcement are largely overcome by shifting to *intermittent reinforcement.* Instead of expressing approval of every act, we use another system to allocate compliments. We may decide to express approval at intervals, such as each time a particular type of task is completed, for instance when an almost-lost customer is recovered.

Another intermittent reinforcement approach is to provide rewards at completely random times. Much of the lure of slot machine gambling comes from the anticipated random windfall. The anticipation or hope of a sudden big reward keeps the players engaged in the "desired behavior"—putting money in the slot. Random rewarding with unexpected bonuses can have this effect.

Under random intermittent reinforcement, workers don't know exactly when they will be rewarded. As long as they hold hope of eventually receiving a reward such as verbal approval, extinction of desired behavior is delayed. If the rewards are too far apart, of course, workers stop producing, unless they are particularly good at working hard today for some far-off but certain-to-be-worthwhile reward. Relatively few workers today are content to "get their reward in heaven."

The best approach is to use continuous reinforcement when new behaviors are being developed and then gradually move to an intermittent schedule, so that the desired performance won't be inadvertently extinguished. In other words, shift the employees' expectations so that longer intervals between reinforcement are seen as normal.

Use Appropriate Praise and Criticism

Sometimes praise is downright embarrassing, and so-called constructive criticism just plain makes you mad. Morrison and O'Hearne have developed an explanation of why praise and criticism seem to have such an on-again/off-again value.[8] These authors suggest that both praise and criticism can be broken down into two types. Type 1 praise consists of statements that have little effect on the performance of the receiver. They are "water off a duck's back." Type 2 praise consists of those statements that might have a positive effect on performance under certain circumstances. There are no guarantees, but these kinds of "attaboys" and "attagirls" might motivate or at least build stronger relationships between the giver and the receiver. Some examples of Type 1 and Type 2 praise are offered in Figure 6-1.[9]

A similar classification of criticism is illustrated in Figure 6-2. Type 1 criticism results in defensiveness and deterioration of performance, while Type 2 criticism is at least potentially constructive in that it *might* result in improved future performance.[10]

Type 1 praise—has little effect on performance of the receiver.	Type 2 praise—may have a positive effect on performance and build an authentic relationship.
1. Generalized praise such as, "You're doing a good job, Charlie." This is meaningless and it generally rolls off the back of the individual without effect. It is often seen as a "crooked" stroke.	1. Specific praise—such as, "Charlie, you did a great job handling that unpleasant customer with a complaint this afternoon." This communicates to the receiver that the boss has actually observed or heard about the praised action.
2. Praise with no further meaning. There is no analysis of why a praised behavior is being commended. This discounts the persons being praised by assuming they will react with higher productivity and better morale merely as a response.	2. Continuing with, "The reason I think it was such a good job is because you acted interested, asked questions, wrote down the facts, asked the customer what she thought we should do to make it right." Analysis of this kind permits the employee to internalize the learning experience.
3. Praise for expected performance, when such praise may be questioned. Mabel, who always gets in on time and is met one morning with, "Mabel, you're sure on time today, you're doing great," from her boss, may wonder what's really going on.	3. Praise for better-than-expected results, for coming in over quota, exceeding the target, putting out extra effort.
4. The "sandwich" system—praise is given first to make the person be receptive to criticism (the real reason for the transaction), which is then followed by another piece of praise, hoping thereby to encourage the person to try harder next time, and feel better about the criticism.	4. Praise, when deserved, is believable when it is given by itself; when mixed with critique it is suspect. Authentic relations develop better when people talk straight. When positive conditional recognition is in order, give it; when critique is deserved, give that. Don't mix the two.
5. Praise perceived by the receiver as given in the nature of a "carrot," mainly to encourage the receiver to work even harder in the future.	5. Praise that is primarily to commend and recognize, and does not seek to put a mortgage on the future.
6. Praise handed out lavishly only when the brass or higher-ups are present. Employees soon recognize the boss is trying to impress superiors with what a good human being he or she really is in dealing with subordinates.	6. Praise given when it is deserved, not just on special occasions, or when it seems to build the image of the praiser to some third party.

Figure 6-1 Ineffective versus Effective Praise

Type 1 criticism—tends to produce a defensive reaction in the receiver and worsen performance.	Type 2 criticism—a type of constructive criticism that may improve performance.
1. Criticism that involves use of the personal "you," e.g., "You're having too many accidents on the lift truck, Bill. What's the matter with you anyway?" It is almost always seen as a discount or put-down by the receiver.	1. Criticism using a situational description, e.g., "Bill, we're experiencing an increase in lift-truck accidents. What's going on?" This indicates the manager is open to looking at all the facts leading to the unfavorable result.
2. Criticism that is unanalyzed. The subordinate then tends to rationalize the criticism as a personal opinion of the manager. Or, the manager is viewed as unable to analyze the problems effectively.	2. Discussion of cause and effect with the unfavorable condition perceived by both as the result of one or more causal factors, one of which might even be the manager!
3. If the situation has been properly assessed, some managers are at a loss to provide coaching necessary for the subordinate to improve. This may be the result of ignorance or lack of competency in deciding on the corrective steps.	3. If steps 1 and 2 above have been properly accomplished, it is important for solutions to be outlined and agreed on. If the subordinate can't do this, the manager must provide, or arrange for, a resource that can develop corrective measures.
4. Critique of an individual in public is not only regarded as humiliating by the subordinate involved, but sometimes even more so by other members of the organization.	4. Individual criticism given in private is usually more acceptable. Saving face is almost as important in Western cultures as it is in the Orient.
5. Criticism given *only* in the interests of the boss (to get the boss recognition, promotion, or raise) or the organization (more profit or status in the marketplace). These may all be legitimate interests, but *authentic* relationships are not likely to develop.	5. Criticism given *also*, or even chiefly, in the interests of the employee (to provide greater competencies, future achievements, or a more secure future with the organization).
6. The manager does all the critiquing, which sets the stage for a Parent-Child [relationship].	6. The subordinate participates in the critiques, even to the point of taking the lead role in defining the unsatisfactory condition, analyzing causes, and suggesting corrective steps.
7. Criticism used as a [calculated] game to justify withholding raises or promotions.	7. Game-free criticism leading toward candor and [authentic interactions].

Figure 6-2 Destructive versus Constructive Criticism

Give Clear Instructions

Two-way instruction giving works best.

Often the most frequent communication managers have with employees is giving orders, directions, or instructions. Although some bosses think of this as one-way, boss-to-subordinate communication, a two-way format is usually far more appropriate.

As managers, we need to know exactly what action we want to result from instructions given. That seems self-evident. Yet this step is occasionally overlooked. When we give an employee instructions to "be more responsive to customers," we may not have a clear picture of exactly what behavior we want to see. Instead we need to mentally clarify our purpose—our reason for giving the order—and then *plan* the best way of creating understanding with the employee.

Use clear, concrete terms when giving instructions.

The phrase "be more responsive" likely has different meanings for different people. Effective instruction givers create a clearer picture of what they want by supplying some details, such as, "You need to greet each customer within ten seconds after they come into the store."

Providing sufficient details and *repetition* are good ways to minimize misunderstandings. The journalist's "who, what, where, when, why, and how" provide a good framework for giving instructions. Be sure you know the answers to each to these before directing someone else. And be sure to encourage questions from the message receiver.

Asking "Do you have any questions?" probably isn't the best technique. The question calls for a yes-or-no response, and many people opt for "no" to avoid showing ignorance. Change the wording to "What questions do you have?" You thereby say to the employee, "It's okay to have questions" and you encourage task clarification. Be sure to pause long enough to let your listeners know you are serious about getting questions from them.

INITIATE AND SUSTAIN AN E-PLUS CUSTOMER LOYALTY STRATEGY[11]

Managers can "operationalize" good intentions into a workable E-Plus strategy by implementing seven key tasks. These need not always be done in the order presented, but several are done concurrently.

Task 1: Orient All Employees

Take steps to ensure that all employees clearly understand the need for cultivating customer loyalty. Teach them about the cost of lost customers, how lost customers lead to lost jobs, why poor service givers pay a psychological price, and why it is in their best interest to develop customer service professionalism. This step is typically done via a series of training sessions.

Also, through training, strive to get employees speaking the same language. Be sure they know the importance of little things, service attitudes, E-Plus and VISPAC, for example.

Begin any strategy by orienting employees.

Task 2: Build Momentum

Conduct regular follow-up departmental meetings after the initial training. Teach basic creativity and group problem-solving skills, and schedule and conduct regular brainstorming sessions to discuss possible new E-Plus ideas. Show individuals and work groups how to set departmental or team goals.

Coordinate the reward system so that the most useful activities get the best rewards. Create a reward committee to determine special bonuses, determine a budget, and define criteria whereby people can win the rewards. Then develop data-gathering forms and processes that give credit for good works. Distribute "Attaboy/Attagirl" cards or small rewards to recognize success immediately.

Task 3: Monitor Customer Expectation and Employee Behavior

Teach "naive listening" techniques to employees. Recognize the value of unhappy customers as sources of improvement ideas. Schedule focus groups—regularly. Record, digest, and keep data and trends analysis.

At the same time, conduct regular shopper surveys to determine the kinds of service people are getting from employees. These should typically be done by independent "shopper services" that provide immediate and specific feedback to employees.

Task 4: Establish Systematic Customer Retention and Follow-Up Efforts

Develop creative customer follow-up techniques. Schedule regular follow-up with mailouts, phone calls, announcements, and special incentives. Try other loyalty builders such as customer photos or customer letters posted on display. Perhaps acknowledge a "Customer of the Month" with recognition.

Task 5: Provide Continuation Training for Employees

Schedule repeat "basic" training for new employees. Also schedule regular continuation training where employees can receive instruction on tasks such as writing customer correspondence, handling difficult people, improving telephone techniques, mastering time and task management, etc.

Task 6: Conduct Ongoing Systems Reviews

Create a task force to review systems. Employ explorer groups to visit competitors or similar businesses that have good ideas. Create a suggestion program to improve systems by announcing and publicizing it, budgeting award money, creating forms, and forming a review committee to evaluate suggestions submitted.

Task 7: Recruit, Develop, and Retain Excellent Employees

Attract and select exceptional service personnel by develop aptitude and attitude testing and interviewing procedures. Proactively invite promising employees from other businesses to join you.

Once people are hired, be sure to clarify promotion criteria and tie these criteria to the customer service reward system. In short, base employee advancement on service attitudes and skills. As part of this process, be sure to conduct meaningful performance reviews with service criteria being measured and factored into the review.

APPLY CONTINUOUS IMPROVEMENT

Customer satisfaction and loyalty present moving targets. What may be seen as the latest, greatest service idea today may quickly become passè. A few years ago, price scanners in supermarkets were rare. Today, we expect them. A few years ago, the idea of offering takeout restaurant service was an innovation. Today it's commonplace. The list of service innovations goes on and the good ones quickly become standard operating procedures.

The outcome of raising the bar of customer expectation is that we all get better service. This is good. But it presents yet another challenge for organizations committed to staying on the leading edge.

In past decades, a number of business buzzwords have emerged to describe various processes for continuously improving. Total Quality Management (TQM), Continuous Quality Improvement (CQI), and a range of similar initialisms were offered as useful procedures for bringing about a constantly improving spiral of product and service quality.

The granddaddy of these approaches is TQM, as originally articulated by W. Edwards Deming. In the years following World War II, Deming, an American statistician with a new management theory, took his ideas to Japan. The Japanese, devastated by the effects of the war, were looking to restructure their economy, and Deming's principles became the blueprint they needed. Now, of course, Japanese products are in demand worldwide.

The Japanese success story made Deming's management theory, Total Quality Management, a phenomenon that got renewed attention in America. With its focus on customer satisfaction, employee empowerment, and product quality, it stirred interest among American managers, from car manufacturers to hospital administrators, and, even more recently, educators.

TQM focuses on customer service, employee empowerment, and product quality.

What Is the Philosophy of TQM?

Although no two businesses use TQM in exactly the same way, its theory rests on two tenets. The first and most important is that customers are vital to the operation of the organization. Without customers, there is no business, and without business, there is no organization. Consequently, it should be the primary aim of any group to keep customers satisfied by providing them with quality products. These ideas are not foreign to most organizations.

What makes TQM unique is its second basic tenet: a call for restructuring management methods to create that quality. TQM proponents urge organizations to turn nearsighted, top-down management "on its head" by involving both customers and employees in decisions. This second tenet, that management needs to listen to nontraditional sources of information in order to institute quality, is based on the belief that people want to do quality work and that they would do it if managers would listen to them and create a workplace based on their ideas.

Managers, in the TQM view, need to become leaders who not only work *in* the system but also *on* the system. A company will see continuous improvement in products only when managers realize that all systems consist of interdependent parts and work to aim all those parts toward a vision of quality, proponents argue. This type of leadership is needed to ensure that product quality improves "constantly and forever" and truly satisfies the customers.

USE TQM TO CREATE AN ENVIRONMENT THAT PROMOTES QUALITY

TQM advocates specific changes that managers need to make if they want to improve their organization's systems. These changes are best described under four categories:

- *Customer relationships.* Customers can be either internal or external to an organization. Just as a customer is the person buying a product in a store, an employee is the customer of management. Managers need to realize that quality work will not be done unless they provide employees with quality products to work with.
- *Employee empowerment.* TQM starts at the top but should permeate throughout the workplace; in fact, it fails without employee involvement. Since workers know more about their jobs than management does, their input is vital to improving the system. It is a manager's responsibility to continually train employees in the methods of TQM, involve them in decisions affecting the company, listen to their suggestions for system changes, and work to implement those changes.
- *Continual gathering and use of statistical data.* Most companies monitor the quality of their products by doing mass inspections that determine how many low-quality items are being produced. TQM calls for monitoring the production process by continually gathering statistical data so that problems can be identified as they are happening instead of when it is too late to solve them. When problems are identified, they should be the focus of discussion, and the groups discussing them should rely on the *data* to institute change instead of randomly assigning blame to individuals or departments.
- *Creating an environment that promotes unity and change.* People need to feel comfortable discussing problems and suggesting solutions. Managers need to work at breaking down barriers between

Service Snapshot

A Fun Way to Start the Week[12]

During her company's Monday morning staff meetings, Susan Groenwald, president of Barter Corp., in Oakbrook Terrace, Illinois, asks employees to share examples of exemplary customer service that the company has provided. Afterward, the 51 workers at the barter network . . . vote for the example they think had the greatest impact on the company's customer service. The winner gets either a cash award or bartered goods. "Rehashing stories gives people a better idea of what good customer service looks like," says Groenwald. "It's also a fun way to start the week." And there's an additional payoff: The meetings arm the company's salespeople with real-life anecdotes to use when they're wooing potential clients.

departments so that interactive discussion can take place. Fear must be eliminated. Also, managers are urged to emphasize teamwork rather than put the focus on competition among individual results.

Cooperative effort is seen as more important than individual competition among employees under TQM.

Is TQM a Fad?

The novelty of TQM and the fact that there are few comprehensive TQM systems have caused many people to label it as a fad. They argue that TQM, like so many management theories before it, is destined to fade into obscurity.

Indeed, there is some indication that quality and service improvement is given lip service more often than it is applied. A study for the American Quality Association revealed that, despite widespread interest, many companies have instituted TQM practices without understanding that it requires a *gradual transformation.* This steady improvement happens only when an organization's leaders have *long-term* vision and dedication to *systematic* change. The primary emphasis in most businesses is still on short-term profits and individual performance, rather than on teamwork and customer satisfaction.

MOVE FROM TQM TO TQS: TOTAL QUALITY SERVICE

Building on the basic TQM philosophy, customer service expert Karl Albrecht describes a model strategy for continuous improvement of customer service, which he calls a Total Quality Service (TQS) model (see Figure 6-3). For each of the elements of Albrecht's original model, I've added the relevant question we need to ask to institute ongoing service improvement in an organization.

1. Marketing and Customer Research: What Do Our Customers Want?

The starting point of the TQS cycle requires that we know what our customers want. In times past, businesses assumed they knew what customers wanted. Henry Ford offered his Model T in any color a customer could want as long as it was black. Later, mass marketing polled customer needs and then gave everybody the product that most people seemed to want. But that was then; this is now. We live in an age when the customer's *individual* wants and needs are considered and acted upon. One large company coined the term "customerize" to allude to its ability to tailor its products to individual customers. (Chapter 9 discusses the future of such personalization.)

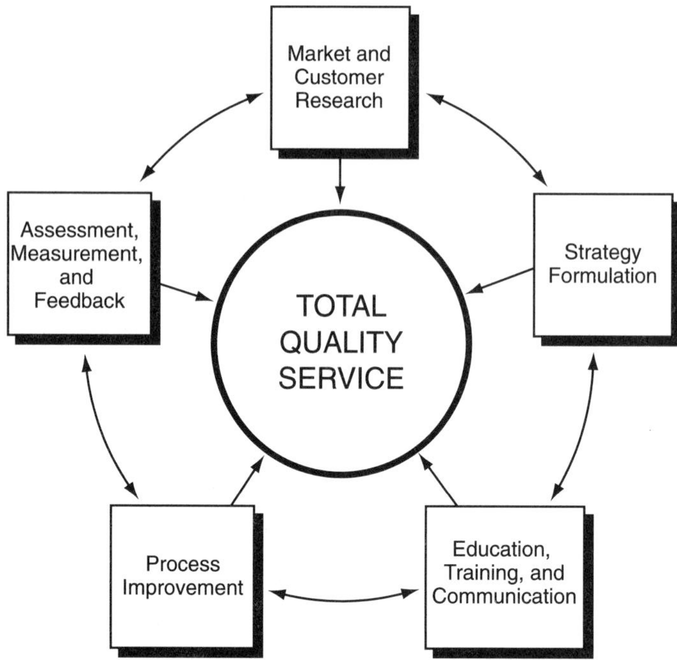

Figure 6–3 The TQS Model for Total Quality Service
© 1988 Karl Albrecht.

Another Look

Peer Coaching: How to Manage When Managers Are Few and Far Between [13]

Once upon a time not very long ago, the average supervisor had responsibility for 5 to 15 people. In today's world of downsized, re-engineered organizations, that figure is closer to 30. The result is, as one frustrated service manager expressed to me: "We don't do management—we do crowd control."

Yet the need for coaching to achieve high-quality service is greater than ever. The solution of choice: peer coaching. Employees of the same level, without the traditional leverage of a boss–subordinate relationship, are being asked to coach one another on substandard and problematic performance.

How's it working? It has its enthusiasts and skeptics.

The negatives are easy to imagine. If you've ever been approached by someone offering to "give you a little feedback," you know the potential problems. On the positive side, peers well trained in the nuances of effective interpersonal communication can be an asset. If you've ever had a colleague pull you aside to warn you the boss is on a tear so you shouldn't bring up the Johnson account, or simply to let you know something was unzipped or stuck between your teeth, you know how valuable peer feedback can be.

Peer coaching—some people prefer to call it peer support—succeeds when the conditions are right and the ground rules clear. Specifically, a successful peer coaching venture requires a supportive environment, awareness of the limits of peer coaching, and tolerance for clumsy communication.

Supportive Environment

If your organization has a history of interdepartmental warfare—marketing and operations only speak through their UN ambassadors, manager-to-manager relations are characterized by jealousy [and] back-biting and nasty barbs at 20 paces, and employees only hear "well done" when they are ordering steak—then peer coaching will fail in your organization in about 2.5 minutes.

If your organization tolerates mistakes as learning opportunities, not time for punishment, peer coaching has a good chance for success.

Awareness of the Limit

Peer coaching is not a panacea. Rather, it is a way of leveraging your skill as a coach by investing some of it in others. It is a supplement rather than a substitute for the coaching you provide. And it definitely is not a way to get out from under the responsibility of dealing directly with employees who have chronic performance problems. That is never a peer responsibility. Peer coaching—all coaching—is about working together with people to build individual and team success.

There are four fundamental axioms to swear allegiance to:

(1) *Peer coaching is not back-seat driving.* Peer coaching is about giving direct, clear feedback and advice, and only doing so with permission or when solicited.

(2) *Peer coaching is not group therapy.* No one in the workplace has a right to probe anyone else's psyche or motivations. The peer coaching process is about "The facts, Ma'am, just the facts." And a limited set of facts—observable, amenable work behavior.

(3) *Helping out is the spirit of peer coaching.* Peer coaching is not a license to blow off steam or give a colleague a piece of your mind. The onus is on the giver to answer three questions before offering Charlie a little help:

- Is Charlie having trouble with a customer, colleague, or situation, or are you uncomfortable with the way Charlie does things?
- Is the problem clearly Charlie's—as opposed to a problem Charlie is involved in but not one he owns?
- If you don't offer to intercede, will the situation cause an irreparable problem for the organization—or for Charlie?

If the answers to all three questions are "yes," you have an obligation to offer help.

Peer coaches respect the "Rule of Once" and the "Right of Refusal":

The Rule of Once: You get to give your feedback and advice once. And only once. The assumption has to be that Charlie heard and understood you. Beyond that, he is free to accept, disregard, or hold your input in abeyance.

The Right of Refusal: You and we and Charlie have a right to say "thank you" and ignore peer input. We even have the right to not listen to peer input.

Tolerance for Clumsiness

Giving counsel and advice to a subordinate is a sweaty-palms situation for many a seasoned manager. Doing it with a peer is even more tense. So a little tolerance goes a long way in creating a climate in which peers can learn to help each other focus their efforts to create a service edge in their organization.

A FINAL THOUGHT

Managing an organization's customer service is a complex task requiring constant vigilance and effort. Managers can accomplish their objectives only when working with and through the efforts of other people. To do so requires tact and skills in communication and motivation. A key to managerial success is to ask pertinent questions and to be open to feedback. The seven tasks of ongoing service improvement (pp. 138–140) provide a way to translate good intentions into a strategy that works.

Summary of Key Ideas

- Basic management functions all play a role in creating and sustaining a customer service strategy.
- Communication plays a central role in all management processes. Problems arise when people receive too little, too much, or poorly expressed information.
- Managing functions that can apply to customer service include developing a service theme, setting service goals, delegating responsibility and authority, recruiting good staff, directing actions, and controlling by checking results against goals.
- Managing by asking tough questions can point to weaknesses in any system.
- Employee motivation can be stimulated by systematic rewarding of appropriate behaviors. Among the most powerful motivators is simply expressing thanks for work well done.
- Praise and criticism must be given judiciously and worded carefully.

- Instructions should be given clearly and repeatedly.
- Seven tasks can effectively translate a slogan into a strategy.

Key Terms and Concepts

Continuous reinforcement
Controlling
Coordinating
Disquieting questions
Intermittent reinforcement
Organizing
Planning
Service themes
Systematic approach to behavior modification
Systems reviews
Three types of poor communication
Total Quality Management (TQM)
Total Quality Service (TQS)

Self-Test Questions

1. What are the four key functions of a manager's job? How do they relate to customer service?
2. What are the three types of poor communication affecting organizations?
3. What are some of the aspects of a good service theme or credo? What are some things to avoid when articulating a service theme or credo?
4. What can a manager do to make the most of a good service theme?
5. Give examples of potentially disquieting questions that can be asked about your organization to determine how well you are doing with customer service.
6. What are the two main schedules of reinforcement? What are the pros and cons of each?
7. What are the seven key tasks that managers can use to turn good intentions into workable customer service strategies?
8. What are TQM and TQS? Give examples.

Activity: Look Inside at Feedback Receptiveness

Take a moment to answer this short self-quiz. Circle a 5 if the statement is almost always true, a 1 if it's almost never true, and some number in between if you prefer to waffle.

A. I feel embarrassed when people point out my mistakes. 5 4 3 2 1

B. I resent people telling me what they think of my shortcomings. 5 4 3 2 1

C. I regularly ask friends and associates I trust to comment on how I am doing. 5 4 3 2 1

D. I know how to offer constructive criticism to others in a sensitive way. 5 4 3 2 1

E. I like having people tell me their reactions to my activities because it helps me adapt my future behavior. 5 4 3 2 1

- *If you scored 4 or 5 on items A and B,* you may be putting up some resistance that could deter you from getting useful feedback. We are normally uncomfortable when we receive harsh or insensitive feedback, but even that can be useful if we wring out the emotion and look at the giver's perspective. Even our worse critic can provide a gift of good advice if we do not allow emotion to blind us. Successful communicators learn to look for good advice even when it's buried under a lot of worthless noise.
- *If you answered 4 or 5 to items C and D,* you are creating a climate in which helpful feedback is expected and accepted. People and organizations that foster such openness can benefit from others' advice.
- *If you answered 4 or 5 to item E,* you are probably a little unusual, but you are on the right track.

Remember, being open to feedback does not mean that you necessarily agree with it. But if you get little or no feedback, you have nothing to sort out, apply, or learn from.

NOTES

[1]S. Nushart, Letter to the Editor, *U.S. News and World Report,* December 11, 1995, p. 6.

[2]R. C. Whiteley, *The Customer-Driven Company: Moving from Talk to Action* (Reading, MA: Addison Wesley Publishing, 1991), p. 27.

[3]L. B. Jones, *The Path: Creating Your Mission Statement* (New York: Hyperion, 1996), p. 4.

[4]See T. W. Firnstahl, "My Employees Are My Service Guarantee," *Harvard Business Review,* July–August 1989, pp. 28–32.

[5]B. Maynard, "How to Manage with Questions," *TeleProfessional,* 209 W.5th Street, Waterloo, IA 50701-5420.

[6]Frequently stating this in different ways, Townsend potently reminded managers in his book—one of the first management books to be a best-seller. R. Townsend, *Up the Organization* (New York: Alfred A. Knopf, 1970), p. 184.

[7]"Productivity Gains from a Pat on the Back," *BusinessWeek,* January 23, 1978, pp. 57–58.

[8]J. H. Morrison and J. H. O'Hearne, *Practical Transactional Analysis in Management* (Reading, MA: Addison-Wesley, 1977), pp. 118–121.

[9]Ibid.

[10]Ibid, pp. 120–121.

[11]This Seven-Step Process is © Paul R. Timm, Ph.D. May not be reproduced without written permission. For further information, contact Paul R. Timm at (801) 378-5682, fax (707) 276-1048, or Email *DrTimm@aol.com.*

[12]"Hot Tip," *Inc.* April 1997, p. 95. Reprinted with permission.

[13]R. Zemke, "Peer Coaching: How to Manage When Managers Are Few and Far Between," *The Service Edge,* July 1996, p. 6. Reprinted with permission of Lakewood Publications.

Foundation Skill

7

Apply Winning Telephone, E-mail, and Web Site Techniques

Achieving Phone and Internet Responsiveness

If you have an unhappy customer on the Internet, he doesn't tell his six friends, he tells his 6,000 friends.

—Jeff Bezos, President, Amazon.com

WHAT YOU'LL LEARN IN THIS CHAPTER

- How to better understand your own attitudes toward telephone courtesy.
- How to recognize and correct the kinds of telephone mannerisms that can lead to customer dissatisfaction.
- How to apply more than 20 techniques to improve your overall telephone effectiveness.
- The pitfalls of ineffective Web page and Internet communication.

The Way It Is

The Frustrations of Unresponsive Telephone Use

Hearing a radio commercial for a concert, I called the number to buy tickets. The number was an easy to remember 888 toll-free number that had the word ARTS as the last four digits. So far, so good. On the first try, the phone rang eight times before I gave up and decided to try again later. My second attempt rang nine times, and then a recorded message gave me another number to call. When I dialed that number an electronic voice put me on hold, after which another recorded voice told me to call the first number I had tried!

Hotel reservations lines, airlines, credit card companies, banks—virtually all companies run their customers through an electronic maze of choices that supposedly make the call more efficient, but often succeed in annoying the caller who simply wants to talk to a human being. I have decided to stay more at Holiday Inns because when I call the reservation line I immediately get a person. I have vowed to avoid companies whose phone service is unresponsive or laborious.

Likewise, shoppers on the Internet will stay with you only a few moments. If your company's Web pages load too slowly or if customers get caught in a loop, they may be lost forever. On numerous occasions I have filled out all the forms to purchase a product on the Net, only to have the system lock up or require me to redo something I've already done. That's when I decide that I don't really need that product. The aggravation isn't worth the potential savings or shopping convenience.

Wise companies are constantly improving phone and Net services, but many are succeeding only at angering or annoying their customers when the customer is ready to buy!

KNOW THE BENEFITS AND DRAWBACKS OF ELECTRONIC COMMUNICATION

The telephone certainly can be, as the ads used to say, "The next best thing to being there." In fact, no business can long survive without a phone. Likewise, today's businesses need e-mail and Web sites. A company without a home page is rapidly becoming an anachronism. But two significant drawbacks to these electronic communicators can almost cancel out their benefits:

1. *Many people have never learned the basics of telephone courtesy and effectiveness.* They've been using the phone since they were children and have never polished their business telephone techniques. What may be everyday casual telephone usage at home may be totally inappropriate for business. The result can be customer dissatisfaction and a severe loss of organizational image and effectiveness.

2. *You cannot see the person you are dealing with.* Electronic media do not permit most nonverbal communication. Without nonverbal cues to reinforce or clarify a message, the listener or Web page viewer may be easily misled or confused.

Phrased another way, each telephone call or Web site "hit" creates interactions whereby people are operating blind—without the visual feedback that helps assign meaning to spoken messages.

To compensate for this lack of visual feedback, we as telephone callers create our own conclusions from what we experience—every nuance conveys subtle messages through timing, tone of voice, word choice, and interruptions. For many people, this ambiguity makes telephone use uncomfortable and even threatening. Although it is a great piece of technology, the telephone can also be frustrating. Web page customers likewise draw conclusions from the graphic appearance of a company's site, its speed, and its ease of use.

Here is a story about a company that lost a customer because it forgot (or never stopped to think about) the drawbacks to telephone communication:

> Garth enjoys working on old cars. A few years ago as he drove to work, he noticed a sports car in an auto dealership's lot. Sensing that such a car would do a lot for his image, Garth decided to inquire about it. He telephoned the dealership and here is how the conversation went.
>
> A receptionist briskly identified the name of the dealership and, just as quickly, commanded, "Hold a minute, please." Fifteen seconds later the receptionist came back on the line and asked, "Can I help ya?" Garth asked to "Speak to someone in used cars, please."
>
> "Just a minute," the receptionist replied.
>
> After a pause, a man's voice said, "Hello?"
>
> "I'd like a little information about the Triumph TR-6 you have on your lot," Garth said.
>
> "Ya mean the red one?"
>
> "Yes. Could you give me some information on that car?"
>
> The male voice hesitated for a moment and said, "I think that's the owner's daughter's car. She's been driving it around. Let me check and see what the deal is on it."
>
> There was a long pause and while Garth waited on hold, another male voice came on the line saying, "Hello? Hello?" to which Garth replied, "I'm already being helped." There was a click as the interrupter hung up without acknowledging Garth's comment.
>
> After a few more minutes, the original salesperson came back on the line and said, "Yeah, I think that's the car the boss's daughter has been driving around. If they sell it, they'll want an arm and a leg for it. I think it's a '75 model."
>
> "Well, would you check and let me know if it's for sale?" Garth asked again, getting exasperated.

"Just a minute, I'll ask the owner," he said as he put Garth on hold again. After a few moments, the salesperson again picked up the telephone and abruptly said, "The owner says it's not for sale."

As Garth began to say, "Thanks for the information," he was cut off in midsentence by the click of the telephone as the man hung up.

Although this sales representative was probably not being intentionally rude, he sure came across that way. Garth was irritated to the point that he would definitely not do business with this dealership.

Another Look

Online Brokerages Flunk Service Test[1]

Online brokers have a lot of work to do to improve customer service. Researchers at Jupiter Communications tested 25 Web sites' rates of response to customers' messages. Among financial services sites, 39 percent responded in one day, while the balance took up to three days or, in the case of 25 percent, never responded. By comparison, 64 percent of retail shopping sites answered e-mails in one day. While businesses are concerned with technology costs, researchers conclude that customer service must get greater priority because new online financial service customers "are mainstream, risk-averse consumers who have far less tolerance for technology issues."

Probes

1. What experience have you had with e-mailing and getting responses from companies?
2. If you were running a company, what standards would you like to see in place? How realistic would this be?

APPLY THESE ACTION TIPS FOR BETTER TELEPHONE USAGE

As we saw in the car dealer example, behaviors that come across as discourteous, disjointed, or intrusive can quickly sour a caller's impression of a company. The remainder of this chapter offers 23 specific tips for improving telephone and Web page effectiveness.[2]

Action Tip 1: Check Your Phone Use Attitudes

The telephone is a powerful tool for sales, information gathering, and relationship building. By receiving and initiating calls, we can accomplish a lot. Yet some people are phone shy. They are hesitant to call others and sometimes hesitant about answering incoming calls.

Check your telephone-use attitudes using the following self-evaluation. It can help you understand some of your attitudes toward using the telephone. It can also help you improve your telephone techniques by showing what you may be doing wrong.

> Your attitudes can impact your telephone effectiveness.

Self-Analysis

How Are Your Phone Usage Skills and Attitudes?

Circle the appropriate letter for each item: N = Never, SL = Seldom, SM = Sometimes, O = Often, A = Always. Then read the instructions at the end of the form.

How Often Do You . . .		*Improvement Goal*
1. Delay calling someone or fail to return a call?	N SL SM O A	____________
2. Answer the telephone with a curt or mechanical greeting?	N SL SM O A	____________
3. Let the phone ring, hoping the caller will give up?	N SL SM O A	____________
4. Save travel time by calling for information ("let your fingers do the walking")?	A O SM SL N	____________
5. End the conversation by summarizing what was agreed upon?	A O SM SL N	____________
6. Solicit feedback about your customer service by phone call?	A O SM SL N	____________
7. Put people on hold for more than a few seconds?	N SL SM O A	____________
8. Have someone else place your calls for you?	N SL SM O A	____________
9. Smile as you speak?	A O SM SL N	____________
10. Speak clearly and in pleasant, conversational tones (no "stage voice")?	A O SM SL N	____________

If you circled a letter in the two right columns for any of the items, your telephone techniques can use improvement. In the space provided to the right of these items, set specific goals for improvement in each area needed.

Action Tip 2: Contact Your Own Company

Many customers get their first impression of you and your company from an electronic visit.

A telephone call or Web page visit is often the first point of contact a person has with an organization. ("You never get a second chance to make a first impression.") Callers create first impressions and draw immediate conclusions about the person's and company's efficiency, communication skills, friendliness, and expertise—all in the first few moments of an electronic visit. In short, your courtesy and effectiveness quickly convey unspoken but important messages to calling customers.

Managers should check on the phone skills of their organization regularly. Have people who know how the phones should be handled call periodically and then prepare a brief report. Likewise, invite inexperienced customers to visit your Web site and let you know what they liked or disliked about it. As always, feedback is the breakfast of champions.

Action Tip 3: Answer Promptly and Be Prepared to Handle Calls

An answer after two rings or less conveys efficiency and a willingness to serve. When the telephone rings longer, callers get the feeling that you are unavailable and that their call is an intrusion. Worse, unanswered callers get the message that you think they are not important.

Be sure that your work area is set up for comfortable and efficient telephone use. Place the telephone at a comfortable spot on your desk or worktable. Keep your frequently called numbers list current and have material you may need to refer to within reach.

Have notepaper, message slips, and pens handy. Use a planner system or desk calendar that has room to jot down notes about conversations you have. Get the caller's name and number as soon as possible and summarize the conversations briefly—especially any commitments you need to follow up on.

Always have note-taking materials handy by the phone.

If you agree to do something for a caller, be sure to write it down and then check it off when completed.

Action Tip 4: Avoid Unnecessary Call Screening

All employees should be encouraged to answer their own telephones unless they are busy in a face-to-face conversation with a customer. Routine screening of calls by a secretary or receptionist often creates resentment in the caller. The constant use of "May I say who is calling?" is recognized as a dodge, an opportunity for people to decide whether they want to talk or not.

Customers get annoyed when there are too many gatekeepers—people who screen calls for others. Here are some other easy-to-adopt tips:

- The appropriate way to answer a business call is to simply state your name or your department and your name.

  Customer support. This is Nancy Chin.

- Calling yourself Mrs., Ms., Mr., or any title may sound a bit self-important.

  Accounting office, Mr. Silvia speaking.

- Some people use just their last name, although this can sometimes confuse callers. A manager friend named Paul Waite found his last-name-only greeting often followed by a very long pause!
- A phrase like "How may I help you?" (or a similar phrase) following your name tells your caller not only whom they are speaking to, but also that you are ready to converse with them.

  When answering another person's telephone, be sure to identify both that other person and yourself.

  Michelle Theron's office. This is Shelly Sampson. May I help you?

  Of course, receptionists would never need to ask who is calling if *callers* would use good business etiquette. Good manners dictate that when we call people, we identify ourselves immediately.

  > As a caller, use good business etiquette by identifying yourself immediately.

  Good morning, Barry Adamson calling. Is Sharon Silverstein there?

  Get in the habit of doing this and you will set a good example for others who may realize the advantage of such courtesy.

Action Tip 5: Use Courtesy Titles

While calling yourself "Mr." or "Ms." may sound stuffy, don't assume that callers prefer to be called by their first names. Use proper titles for the people to whom you refer. If in doubt as to whether to use a first name, call the person by the more formal "Mr." or "Ms." If they prefer the more informal first name, they will say so. It is better to be initially a little too formal than overly familiar.

Titles and formality can create credibility. If you refer to other professionals, refer to them formally. You'd be a bit thrown off if a medical doctor introduced himself as, "Hi, I'm Larry, your brain surgeon." Even if your organization has an informal culture, don't assume that others do.

Action Tip 6: Thank People for Calling

"Thank you" is the most powerful phrase in human relations. Express appreciation regularly. Some companies use it as a greeting: "Thank you for calling Avis." A "thanks for calling" at the end of a conversation is also a strong customer satisfaction booster. It reassures customers that you are interested in serving and that their call was not an intrusion.

A "Thank you for visiting" note on a Web site can convey the same appreciation, especially if the site visit was a good one.

Action Tip 7: Keep Your Conversation Tactful and Businesslike

Nothing turns off a customer or caller like poor wording. I've had experiences when upon telling people my name, they say, "Who?" rather abruptly. Few things make a caller feel less appreciated. If you didn't catch the name, ask politely, "I'm sorry, I didn't get your name, sir. Would you repeat it?"

Keep your comments positive and oriented toward solving the caller's problem or concern. Don't just toss the ball back when you can't immediately help. Don't say anything that makes people or your organization look unprofessional or uncaring.

Here are some other dos and don'ts:

DON'T SAY	DO SAY
Who is this?	May I ask who's calling?
What's your name?	I'm sorry, but I didn't get your name.
What do you need?	How can I help you?
Speak up, please.	I'm sorry, I can't hear you. Could you speak a little louder?
Well, I wasn't the one you talked to.	I'm sorry Ms. James, someone else . . .
He's out to lunch.	Mr. Barringer is away from the office for about one hour. Can I ask him to call you back?
You'll need to call our billing office.	That information is available in our billing office. I'll be happy to connect you. (Or shall I ask someone in billing to call you back?)
Sorry, I can't help you with that.	I don't have that information here. May I have someone from our quality service department give you a call?

There's nothing I can do about that.	I'll put that on my calendar for next Tuesday and I'll check on your request again then. Then I'll call you back.

Action Tip 8: Speak Clearly and Distinctly

Hold the telephone mouthpiece about a half-inch from your lips. Whether you answer with your name, the company name, or the department name, speak clearly and distinctly. For example, carefully say:

> Good morning, Primo Computer Service or hello, this is KJQQ radio, scheduling department [followed by your name]. [Separate the words with tiny pauses.]

Even if you say these words a hundred times a day, resist the temptation to get lazy or to repeat the greeting in a mechanical, unfriendly manner. Remember that each caller hears your greeting just once, even though you have said it many times. Make it fresh and sincere.

Action Tip 9: Speak Naturally and Comfortably

Talk to your caller as you would to a friend. Use warm, friendly voice tones and natural, spontaneous reactions. If callers say something humorous, laugh. If their tone of voice suggests tension or even anger, it may be appropriate to comment on that: "You sound upset; is there something I can do to help?"

A strong, clear voice is a tremendous asset. It conveys confidence and high credibility. But even if you are not gifted with the voice of a professional broadcaster, a person can do things with the voice that create and hold listener interest.

The key to holding interest is *variation* in the voice. People cannot pay attention to something that does not change. But we do perk up when speakers adjust their voices. The three things any speaker can vary are pitch, loudness, and rate.

Pitch is almost a musical quality: the place on a musical scale where the voice would be. Male speakers tend to have more trouble varying pitch than females. The problem, of course, is that too little variation in pitch sounds like a monotone. In a word, it is boring.

Another problem is that people try to force their voices into a different pitch. By artificially speaking too low or too high, we create a stage voice that sounds phony. Use your natural range, but experiment with broadening that range, too.

Some speakers do not want to risk much variation. They fear sounding silly. Failing to vary pitch is like throwing away one of your most useful tools for effective communication. Listen carefully to good radio or TV announcers, comedians, or other entertainers. You will find that they vary their pitch a lot. Try pushing your range of pitch outward a bit. Go a little higher and a little lower than you typically do, and you will find listeners more interested in what you have to say.

Action Tip 10: Do Not Allow "Dead Air"

Broadcasters call the awkward gaps when nothing is being broadcast "dead air." Listeners have no idea what is going on and often change stations if the silence persists. The same can happen with a telephone call.

If you need to transfer a caller, look up information, or read material, *tell callers what you are doing*. Remember, they cannot see you. Use statements such as these to reassure your callers that you are still with them:

> I will transfer you to Mr. Kovak now. He can get you that information. One moment please.
>
> I understand your concern. Ms. Jessop in our billing department can best help you with that. May I put you on hold for a moment? I will see if she is in.
>
> I'm reviewing your account now, Mr. Jenson. Let me just check a few figures and I can give you that information in a moment.

Putting people on hold can be annoying to callers, but you can reduce this annoyance by telling them what you are doing and why.

Always acknowledge comments audibly. Be sure to react to your caller's conversation. Since your callers can't see you and don't receive visual feedback from you, they must rely on your spoken feedback—on what you say—to determine whether you understand what is being said.

By frequently saying "Yes," "I see," "Uh-huh," or "I agree," you are providing the needed feedback. Don't let caller comments go unacknowledged.

The Web page equivalent of dead air happens when material loads too slowly. Keep current with the latest technology that gives you a quickly moving, efficient Web site. Stamp out dead air.

Action Tip 11: Take Messages Cheerfully and Accurately

Be willing to take messages for others. Keep a note pad handy to record key words and phrases. Read the message back to the caller to be sure it is accurate. Then be sure to pass the message to the right person. Most organizations use message forms like the one on page 161. Fill out the form completely and legibly.

As you fill out a message slip, be complete. To avoid possible communication problems, it is especially important to:

1. *Get the full name and correct spelling.* If you don't understand it clearly, ask callers to spell their names for you. Let them know why you are asking for the spelling by saying something like, "I want to make sure your message is accurate. Will you spell your name?"
2. *Ask for the name of the organization, if appropriate.* The best reason for this is that it may give the message receiver a hint as to the nature of the call. It can also be a way of double-checking if there is a mistake with the number.
3. *Get the full telephone number, including the area code for long distance.* If the caller says, "She has it," you can say politely, "I know she can get back to you even faster if I jot your number down with your message."
4. *Ask for a message.* If the caller doesn't volunteer any specific message, it saves on the callback time if you ask, "Is there any information you would like to leave that may be helpful to Ms. Jones when she calls you back?"
5. *Say "thank you" and assure the caller.* Tell the caller that you will give the receiver the message as soon as he or she is available. Say this with assurance.
6. *Note the time and date the message was taken.*
7. *Add your initials to the message slip in case there are any questions.*

Action Tip 12: Smile

Picture the person you are talking with and treat him or her as though you were face to face with a friend. Be pleasant. Be concerned. Be helpful. Physically smiling somehow comes through the telephone line via your voice tones.

Keep a mirror by the telephone to remind yourself to smile. It really does come through to the caller.

Action Tip 13: Be Sure the Conversation Is Finished Before You Hang Up

If you initiated the call, take the responsibility for ending it. Use conclusion words such as, "Thank you for your help" or, "That is just what I needed."

If you received the call, be sure the caller is finished. In our opening story, Garth was about to ask the salesperson if the dealership had any other sports cars available, but was cut off before he could.

To ____________________ ☐ URGENT

Date ____________ Time ____________ A.M. / P.M.

WHILE YOU WERE OUT

From ____________________

of ____________________

Phone ____________________
Area Code · Number · Extension

Telephoned	☐
Came to see you	☐
Returned your call	☐

Please call	☐
Wants to see you	☐
Will call again	☐

Message ____________________

Signed ____________________

Fill out telephone message slips fully so the receiver will be ready to return the call.

Action Tip 14: Make Your Greeting Message Efficient

When you are not available, use an answering machine or voice mail to capture messages. Keep your greeting message current, brief, and not too clever. Messages like the following usually work fine:

> You have reached 555-1131. We cannot take your call now. Please leave a message at the tone. (Note: This message does not identify who you are and may provide privacy and security.)
>
> This is Acme Manufacturing's Warehouse. Our business hours are from 8 A.M. to 6 P.M. Monday through Friday. Please leave a message.
>
> Thank you for calling NuHousing, Inc.—your mobile home leader. Please leave a message at the tone and we will get back to you as soon as we can. Thank you.

Recorded messages may also ask for specific information from callers. ("If you have your account number available, please leave it so we can respond to your request more quickly.") Do not, however, ask for too much. Also, assure the caller that you will return the call.

When you leave a message on another person's machine, be sure to state the following:

- Your name (spoken clearly and spelled if necessary).
- Time and day of your call.
- A brief explanation of why you are calling.
- Your phone number.
- When you can be reached.

Here are two examples:

> This is Jim Steadman calling. It's 7 P.M. Friday. I have a question about your new Wave Runners. Please call me at 555-3077 after 10 A.M. Saturday.
>
> This is Raul Sanchez. That is spelled S-A-N-C-H-E-Z. I am interested in your job opening for an experienced night programmer and would like to arrange an interview. I have six years' experience with a company like yours. Please call me at 555-0819 after 6 P.M. today, Thursday the 4th. Thank you.

Action Tip 15: Learn to Use Your Phone's Features

The wonderful world of telephone technology is constantly coming up with new features. Unfortunately, like the 80 percent of people who have no idea how to program a VCR, many businesspeople haven't learned to use the many tricks available through their phone systems.

A recent study of IBM customer complaints found that customer dissatisfaction with the firm's phone call handling stemmed from two general classes:

1. The inability of employees to use the features of telephone and voice mail systems, and
2. Shortcomings in treating customers with the highest degree of courtesy.

IBM responded to these concerns by providing additional training for all employees. Such training boosted customer satisfaction with the firm's telephone responsiveness dramatically.[3]

If you are uncertain about the use of your telephone system's features, call the manufacturer company. They will be happy to have a representative teach you how to use the system. After all, it is in their best interest to have you using the equipment fully, so that they have a satisfied customer.

Action Tip 16: Keep a Constant Flow of Information

If you spend a sizable percentage of your day on the phone, consider getting a headset rather than having to hold the receiver to your ear. Likewise, if you find that you frequently have to step away from the phone for information while the caller holds, consider using a cordless phone that allows you to continue talking while you move about.

Also, use the hold button carefully. What may seem to you like a brief hold, can seem awfully long to a caller. Even if your phone system plays music, callers get pretty upset after 30 seconds or so. Try timing the next time you are put on hold. A minute can seem like an eternity. Keep voice contact or pick up every 15 to 20 seconds to let callers know that you haven't forgotten them. If you anticipate a fairly long hold time, offer to call back or at least prepare callers by saying that this will require several minutes to complete. Then give them the option of holding or awaiting a callback.

Action Tip 17: Plan Your Outgoing Calls or E-mail for Efficiency

Although small talk is sometimes useful to create a good relationship with callers, strive to make business calls concise without being curt or abrupt. This can be especially important when using cellular telephones because charges can be high for "air time"—the time you use the cellular network. Even for local calls, charges can run 50 cents per minute or more, depending on the time of day.

When placing a business call or writing an e-mail, plan what you will say, preferably in writing. Jot down some notes that include:

1. The purpose of your message.
2. A list of information you need to get or give.

Be sure to identify yourself and the reason for your message early in the conversation. Businesspeople do not like playing "Guess who!" or "Guess what!" A good way to kick off a typical call would be to say:

> Hello. This is Tina Watson calling from Unicorn Corporation. Is Marilyn Smith in?

Once connected with Ms. Smith, say:

> Hello, Ms. Smith. This is Tina Watson with Unicorn Corporation. I need to get some information about your recent catalog order. Is this a good time for you to talk?

Notice that the caller identifies herself, previews what she needs to discuss, and also asks about the person's readiness to talk. If the person is busy and cannot give your call full attention, this is a chance to offer to call you back.

When you need to return calls to people who have called you, schedule them at times they are likely to be in. Be aware of probable lunch hours and long-distance time differences. If you do not, you are likely to play that dreaded game: telephone tag. You keep returning calls and just missing the person who is trying to call you.

Time your callbacks for efficiency. Be specific about when you plan to call a person back. Vague statements like "I'll get back to you on that" may create unrealistic expectations. The caller expects to hear from you within 15 minutes while you meant two or three hours. Instead, say, "I'll can you back between one and two this afternoon" and, of course, do it during that time frame.

Action Tip 18: Don't Let the Telephone Interrupt an Important Live Conversation

One of the pet peeves of many customers is having their discussion with a businessperson interrupted by a phone call. If you are talking live to someone, do not assume that the phone call is more important or should be accorded priority.

If you must take the call, always excuse yourself. When you determine what the call is about, inform the caller that you have someone with you now and that you will be happy to call back at a specified time.

Action Tip 19: Keep Callers on Track

If a caller digresses into chit-chat or nonessential conversation, use a bridging technique to get back on track. This often calls for some creativity, but give it a try.

If your caller says:
I get really sick of this gloomy weather around here. It really gets to you after a while, don't you think?

You might say:
Well, one way we can brighten your day is to get this billing problem straightened out (or get that new recliner ordered for you, or give you the information you've been wanting).

If your caller says:
How about those Buffalo Bill's last week. They never looked tougher. Flutie is still the best QB in the league, don't you think?"

You might say:
They were good. I hope I can get your "bills" straightened out for you real soon (or which reminds me, we need to be looking long and deep into your financial plan, or let's tackle this order for you).

If your caller says:
I really appreciate your help with the Special Olympics last weekend. Your company is a big help.

You might say:
Well thank you, Ms. Knowaki. I hope I can help you find that widgit you called about too. Let's see. Here it is . . .

If your caller wants to chat on and on, take charge:

Mrs. Customer, let me summarize what you've said and then if there is anything else you need to tell me, you can fill in.

When callers are exceptionally upset, let them get it all out before you attempt to interrupt. An interruption just makes them angrier. As they describe their anger, offer sympathetic comments that let them know that you are still listening: "I see." "Wow, that doesn't sound like we treated you very well." "I know how upsetting that can be."

Action Tip 20: Handle the Upset Caller with Tact and Skill

We discussed customer recovery in Chapter 3. Here are some additional tips for recovering upset callers. First, recognize that handling upset or difficult people entails two steps:

Step One: Understand Why They Are Upset or Difficult

The three common root causes of anger or frustration are peoples' feelings that:

1. They are not valued or important.
2. They are helpless.
3. "It" just isn't fair.

We have all experienced these feelings at some time. Be empathic and recognize that these don't make the caller a bad person but rather a person who is having an unpleasant experience. Try to put yourself in his or her position.

Step Two: Defuse the Anger or Frustration with a Series of Statements or Questions

1. *Help me to understand.* This encourages them to explain why they are upset. Don't try to defend or argue with their perceptions; they know what they feel, even if it doesn't make a lot of sense to you. Then let them know that you empathize . . . .
2. *I can understand why you would feel that way.* Do not say "I know *exactly* what you mean" because you probably don't. Instead, convey that you have an idea of what they might be feeling. Then ask . . .
3. *What would be a good solution from your point of view?* This begins to shift the conversation away from the venting of emotion and toward solution seeking.

Strive to have callers share the responsibility for finding a reasonable solution to the problem being experienced. When they have made a proposal or suggested an idea that might work, you can begin a negotiating process that can lead to a reconciliation—and cooling off.

Action Tip 21: Bring the Conversation to a Pleasant but Efficient Close

It can be tempting to talk on with friendly people, but others may be waiting to talk to you and other work awaits. Try some of these techniques for tactfully closing a conversation even when the caller seems to want to go on:

1. *Summarize the call and what has been decided.* Say, "Let me go over what we decided to do" or "Let me summarize the process for you." Spell out what has been done: "I closed that account and transferred $1,000 to your new fund." "That is all you need to do for now. It has been taken care of."
2. *Speak in the past tense.* "As we discussed." "That was all the information I needed." "I'm glad that you called."
3. *Say "Thank you for calling."* This is a universal clue that the conversation is over.
4. *End the call positively.* "I've enjoyed talking with you, Mr. Blanko."

Action Tip 22: Always Ask, "Is This a Convenient Time to Talk?"

Too many callers burst into their message when the person being called may be involved in something else. If there is any possibility that the person may be busy, ask if this is a good time before you begin.

If asked that question and it really isn't a good time, let the caller know and arrange another time to talk that would be more convenient.

This tip also holds if you don't have information you may need to answer a caller's questions. Be honest and tell him so. Then arrange a callback.

Action Tip 23: Work Consistently to Improve Your Electronic Communications

Good telephone skills are essential for career success in almost every field. Make it an ongoing effort to get feedback about your skill level. Take the opportunity to attend seminars or view training videos that teach new and specialized skills.

If you supervise other people, don't hesitate to critique their telephone skills. Be frank with them if some things they are doing are inconsistent with the tips in this book. Remind them of the critical importance—to the company and to their professionalism—of good telephone skills.

Be observant. Listen carefully to both the spoken and unspoken messages that may be sent to your callers. Remember that when you use the telephone, your communication channel is limited. There are no visual cues being sent; your callers can't see you. So help them "see" you in the best possible light by using winning telephone techniques.

For Internet communication, constantly evaluate your Web site and modify it as necessary. Ask customers to comment on the site and its functions. Change anything that seems annoying or inefficient. A Web site should never be considered "final." It should constantly evolve.

A FINAL THOUGHT

More and more customers are using electronic media to access businesses. Telephone and e-mail usage is increasingly important to modern organizations. It makes sense for organizations and people to be aware of the advantages as well as the limitations of these media. People who have a poor experience with you, over the phone or Net, are highly unlikely to become loyal customers.

Clearly, poor telephone and Web site techniques can have a dramatic impact on a company's success. Winning techniques build stronger relationships with customers and other people important to the organization. And employees who master such techniques are particularly valuable to the company.

Summary of Key Ideas

- Understanding our own attitudes toward telephone use and courtesy can help us become more effective in dealing with customers via electronic media.
- Ineffective telephone mannerisms can lead to poor first impressions and customer dissatisfaction.
- The application of 23 techniques improves overall telephone effectiveness.
- Web sites and Internet contact must run efficiently and be constantly reassessed to maintain excellent customer contact and responsiveness.

Key Terms and Concepts

Call screening
Courtesy titles
"Dead air"
Electronic communication
Loudness
Phone use attitudes
Pitch
Rate
Telephone mannerisms
Visual cues (lack of)

Self-Test Questions

1. Compare and contrast the benefits and drawbacks of electronic communication.
2. How do our phone use attitudes affect our telephone techniques?
3. How can we best prepare our physical environment to handle calls?
4. What is call screening? Why should its unnecessary use be avoided?
5. How can you know whether to address a caller by a courtesy title or by first name?
6. What three things can speakers vary in their voice to keep the listener's attention?
7. What is "dead air"? How can it be avoided?
8. What are some important steps to apply to message taking?
9. What kind of information should you have on your answering message? What kind of information should you provide when speaking to answering messages?
10. How can learning to use your phone's features enhance electronic communication?

11. How can planning your outgoing calls result in better efficiency?
12. What are the two important steps required in handling the irate caller?

Activity 1: Identify the Errors in Garth's Call

Reread the story of Garth's call to the car dealership on page 152. Then describe four or more telephone use problems that probably led to Garth's irritation and his decision not to do business with that dealer.

Problem 1: ______________________________

Problem 2: ______________________________

Problem 3: ______________________________

Problem 4: ______________________________

Most people who hear of this incident quickly identify the unspoken message projected loud and clear by the dealership: This caller (and potential customer) isn't particularly important. Perhaps this is because the car in question isn't for sale (and the shortsighted salesperson can't see any advantage to be gained by being polite), or perhaps their telephone usage is hopelessly rude and unprofessional. They've forgotten or have never learned the basics of telephone courtesy.

Whatever the reason, the outcome is the same: a caller who has been treated poorly and harbors resentment against this business.

Activity 2: Try Rewording for a Better Tone

See if you can rephrase the following statements to make the wording positive and tactful. Also, strive to solve the caller's concern as efficiently as possible:

1. Bill is out playing golf again. I doubt that he'll be back in the office today.

   ____

   ____

2. Sarah went to the restroom and then is going to lunch for about an hour or so.

   ____

   ____

3. Who did you say you were?

____

____

4. You say you've been trying to get through? When did you try?

____

____

5. Whom are you holding for?

____

____

6. This is Bobby. What do you need?

____

____

7. Hey, sorry about that. I got backed up and couldn't call you back.

____

____

8. We don't do that kind of work here.

____

____

9. Try again after five, okay?

____

____

10. Sally used to work here but we let her go. Maybe I can help.

____

____

Activity 3: Hear the Difference

1. Try this simple exercise to demonstrate how voice inflection can change the meaning of what you say. Repeat out loud the following sentence, first just using your normal voice.

   Henry didn't show up for work today.

   Now restate the same sentence:

   - Put surprise in your voice!
   - Make it sound like a secret.
   - Turn it into a question.

2. Next, try saying the following sentence with the emphasis on a different word each time:

   I think Doris can do that.

   When you emphasize the word *I,* the unspoken message may be, "*I* think she can do it, although maybe no one else thinks so."

   When you emphasize the word *think,* it conveys an unspoken message of uncertainty.

   Listen for other possible unspoken messages as you emphasize *Doris, can,* and *that.*

   Notice how these subtle changes in voice and emphasis can convey widely different meanings.

Activity 4: Your Answering Machine Greeting

Take a moment to plan your answering machine message tape. Make it pleasant and encourage listeners to leave a message, but also be efficient.

Activity 5: Critique this Call

The following situation describes a fairly commonplace business telephone conversation. In the space provided at the right, critique what is going on. Note both effective and ineffective techniques used by each speaker.

The Story	***My Critique***
Diane: Good morning, marketing department. This is Diane. May I help you?	________________
Bobbi: Hi, is this marketing? Oh good. I need to find out some information about your future seminar schedule. Let me see now . . . [pause] there are several cities where our people might want to attend. [pause] I've got a list here somewhere. I know Cleveland is one . . .	________________ ________________ ________________ ________________ ________________
Diane: We do have seminars scheduled for Cleveland, but which programs are you interested in?	________________ ________________
Bobbi: I'm not real sure. My boss just asked me to get a schedule from you. Don't you have a secretary training class?	________________
Diane: Yes. In fact we have three professional secretaries programs. One is for the new employee and another for advanced—those with two years' experience or more—and one that focuses on word processing.	________________ ________________ ________________ ________________

Bobbi: Oh, good. Oh, here it is. I found my list of cities. The Cleveland, Buffalo, Denver, and Biloxi offices all seem interested. They said they saw a brochure about your company.

Diane: Do you have one of our brochures?

Bobbi: No, I haven't seen it.

Diane: Okay. Here's what I think we should do. I will send you a brochure with the list of cities and dates for our seminars. Let's see. We will be in Cleveland, Buffalo, and Denver in the next two months, but not Biloxi. Perhaps there is a nearby city your Biloxi people could go to. I'll send you a complete list and you can handle the registration by phone or fax. Will this be satisfactory?

Bobbi: Great. Sounds perfect. You will include pricing and everything, I assume?

Diane: I sure will. And I know your people will love the seminars. They're really neat. Now, can I get your name and address? I'll get this information into the mail today . . .

Probes

1. What was accomplished by Diane's greeting?

2. What did Bobbi fail to do in her opening remarks?

3. What information did Bobbi need to make this a successful conversation?

4. How well did Diane handle the call?

5. What would you do differently if you were Bobbi? If you were Diane?

6. Did you notice the ways Diane reassured the customer? Why is that important?

7. How was the overall efficiency of this call?

Activity 6: Getting Back on Track

See if you can tactfully get the conversation back on track when your caller digresses. Write a bridging comment that might help you do so:

1. My daughter is getting married on November 19, so things have been pretty hectic here at home.

   ___

   ___

2. With all the playoff excitement, I haven't been able to concentrate on getting this accounting problem taken care of. Can you believe that comeback in last night's game?

   ___

   ___

3. The kids are growing too fast. Just yesterday my youngest asked for a new guitar so he can join a rock band. He's only 13.

   ___

   ___

4. That reminds me of the time I made my first birdie playing golf. It was a cool but clear day and I was playing pretty lousy until the 13th hole—lucky 13.

   ___

   ___

NOTES

[1]Transmitted online from *Internet Daily,* sponsored by CBS MarketWatch, September 1, 1999.

[2]Many of the ideas in this chapter are adapted from the author's videotape training program and book, *Winning Telephone Techniques* (Chicago: JWA Video, 1997). This program can be purchased through JWA Video by calling 312-829-5100.

[3]M. Estabrooke and N. F. Foy, "Answering the Call of Tailored Training," *Training,* October 1992, p. 85.

Foundation Skill

8

Use Written Messages

Share Information with Customers in Written Documents

Some people would rather eat a bar of soap than write a business letter.

—Author

WHAT YOU'LL LEARN IN THIS CHAPTER

- Build customer loyalty with unexpected thank-you notes and goodwill messages.
- Use written media to get publicity and to build customer awareness.
- Effectively share information with customers in written documents and e-mail messages.

The Way It Is

Follow-Up Notes Are Good Business

When I was a manager trainee in my first job out of college, I sent a letter to the college recruiter who had hired me. The letter was brief: I simply said how much I enjoyed working for the company and how he had helped me. I received a call from him a few days later. He thanked me for the letter and commented that, of all the trainees he had worked with, I was the only one who had written to him in this way.

Interestingly, a short while later he was instrumental in my getting promoted to a better position.

Best-selling author Harvey Mackay talks about "short notes [that] yield long results" in his book, *Swim with the Sharks without Being Eaten Alive.* He comments on how few people send follow-up notes to customers, even those who have made a major purchase, like a car. Another glaring omission of many people interviewing for a job is the follow-up thank-you note to the interviewer.

Mackay cites many successful people who constantly send out short but effective notes with messages like "I want you to know how much I enjoyed our meeting/interview/your gift/your hospitality" or "Congratulations on your new house/car/tennis trophy."

The moral of the story: Don't hesitate to let people know that you appreciate them, and *do it in writing.* Don't worry about formality or business protocol. Often a handwritten note, written conversationally, works fine.

A professor friend of mine recently asked members of an executive education business class this question: "How many of you have written a business document for your job within the past 24 hours? The past week?" The answer was surprising. Out of the 62 working professionals in the class, only one had written within the past day and four within the past week. The professor's point is that business communication, with its many media choices, is quite different now than in the past and that many managers seldom, if ever, write a paper document. The other point, however, is that when we do put forth the effort to write a document, it has the potential for being noteworthy in the mind of the reader. The idea that someone would take the time and effort to write can have a dramatic effect on people.

Thank-you letters are routinely sent by businesses that sell high-priced items like cars, trucks, appliances, furniture, and the like. But companies are increasingly recognizing the value of the thank-you note to buyers of even lower-priced items. I recently received a note of appreciation from the owner of the athletic shoe store where I'd just purchased some jogging shoes.

Why do this? Because such correspondence can form the beginning of an ongoing business relationship. It tells customers that they are important to you and that you are available to serve further. Writing notes to customers is an often overlooked way to create that all-important one-to-one relationship. In this chapter we consider the power of such letters that are called goodwill messages.

APPLY THESE TIPS WHEN USING GOODWILL MESSAGES

A goodwill note or letter is one you write even though you don't have to. Many people, by failing to send goodwill messages, overlook an excellent opportunity to promote good feelings toward and within their organization. Applying the power of written communication can quickly set one organization apart from most others. So the first tip is . . .

Just Do It

Few things make an employee (an internal customer) feel better than to receive a brief letter of appreciation, congratulations, sympathy, or concern from the boss or a coworker. It only takes the writer a minute, yet it can help to develop good employee relations. Likewise, customers who receive sincere, personal messages from people they do business with will likely harbor more favorable feelings toward that person and organization.

Be Original

Sending Christmas cards used to be an effective way to plant your company's name before current and prospective customers. "People can't help feeling warmly about you," says John Kahl, president and CEO of Manco Inc., a $60-million marketer of a line of tapes, weather stripping, and mail supplies. But, says Kahl, there is only so much warmth to go around. So many companies now send cards that yours can get lost in the shuffle. That's why he has added other, less popular holidays to his mailing roster: Thanksgiving, St. Patrick's Day, and the Fourth of July, to be specific. "It's a good way to break through," he claims.

To heighten interest, he has the cards designed in-house so they're different from run-of-the-mill cards. "People open them up just to see what the next one will look like," says Kahl, whose mailing list includes some 30,000 people. "It's a much more personal way to reach them."

> Look for opportunities to send a variety of written messages to customers, internal and external. Few things better set you apart from the many people and organizations that fail to do so.

USE SALES FOLLOW-UP LETTERS

The following letter is sent to customers who buy automobiles from a Chevy dealer. As you'll see, it combines goodwill with some useful instructions.

Christensen
CHEVROLET / BUICK / GEO

Jan 6, 1999

Paul R. Timm
81 E. Cyprus St.
Orem UT 84058

Dear Paul:

We appreciate your business and the opportunity to work with you. Below is some information you will find helpful.

We normally receive your license plates about four weeks after all the paperwork from the sale is completed. We will send you a postcard when the plates are ready to be picked up here at our Cashier's window.

The title is issued by the state government and will be sent directly to the firm that loaned the money for the vehicle. If you paid cash, the title should reach you about two months following the completion of the paperwork from the sale.

Our Service and Parts Departments are open Monday through Friday for regular service. A courtesy bus is available at no charge in the Provo-Orem area Monday-Friday. Please call when your car needs servicing to make an appointment in order to minimize delays.

Chevrolet, Buick and Geo all send out important survey forms to a percentage of our customers during the first month after the sale and again at 5 months. We strive to make our customers *very satisfied.* If you are not, please let us know first. When you receive a survey form, please take the time to fill it out and return it in the envelope provided.

We care about you as our customer and look forward to a continued business relationship. Our goal is to be deserving of your future business.

Sincerely yours,

Mike Echevarria

Mike Echevarria
General Manager

Self-Analysis

Critique the Letter

You can learn a lot from the examples of others. Get into the habit of critiquing business letters you receive. Create a list of your likes and dislikes. Start with the letter from the Chevy dealer. List five likes and dislikes, and then summarize what you'd do differently if you were to write such a letter.

Likes	Dislikes
1. ______________	1. ______________
2. ______________	2. ______________
3. ______________	3. ______________
4. ______________	4. ______________
5. ______________	5. ______________

Please remember that there is no absolute, *right* way to create such a message. Its effectiveness ultimately depends on the receiver's interpretation.

USE ROUTINE INFORMATIVE MESSAGES

Routine messages answer simple questions. Typical examples are letters that ask for or offer explanations or that order a product being advertised. The receiver of such a message is likely to be happy to get it. For the receiver, it answers questions, and for the sender it presents an opportunity for relationship building.

> Routine informative messages answer simple questions or make easy requests.

Routine letters and memos are an essential part of business. For many companies they represent the bulk of business writing. Some common topics for routine writing include announcements, inquiries about products or services, letters granting a request, letters of introduction, etc.

Here is an example of an announcement letter:

Bronson Security Systems

KEEPING AN EYE ON YOUR ASSETS

Mr. Blaine Wilson, President
NuWay Technology
12777 Highway 50
Orlando, FL 27002

Dear Mr. Wilson:

At Bronson Security Systems, we're always looking for better ways to serve your needs for plant security. I think we've found another in Arnold (Bucky) Corridini.

Bucky has joined us as Coordinator of Surveillance Services. He will help us maintain and improve the high standard of quality service you've come to expect from Bronson.

Of all the candidates we considered for this position, we found Bucky offered the best combination of ability, enthusiasm, and professionalism. Most important, he is the kind of person we want working on your account at NuWay Technology—the best.

I'm confident you'll see this valuable addition to our staff as further evidence that we are committed to our clients. I've asked Bucky to personally introduce himself to you within the next week. If there's anything he or I can do for you, please call.

Thank you for doing business with us.

Sincerely,

Guido Lambini

Guido Lambini, President
Bronson Security Systems

This sample gives you a feel for the types of written messages that can be used to build customer relationships. Think about how you might change the tone or content to better fit your personal communication style. Remember, appearing in print does not mean it is perfect for all occasions and audiences. Your personal touch can dramatically improve it. Communication is an art and you are the artist.

> Get into the habit of critiquing the letters you receive. Then develop your own style.

USE THREE GENERAL GUIDELINES FOR ROUTINE MESSAGES

Writers should apply three principles when writing routine letters:

- Be direct.
- Be complete.
- Be polite.

A writer can do little to destroy the effectiveness of a blatantly good-news message. The intent is to tell readers something they are glad to hear or, at worst, are neutral toward. People value efficiency of communication. Keep goodwill letters brief, although not abrupt, and to the point.

Service Snapshot

The Ultimate Electronics Difference

Bill decided to buy his compact disc player at Ultimate Electronics. He'd heard positive things about the store and decided to give it a try. He had this to say of the experience:

> I personally get very frustrated when I go into a store and I have to find someone to help me. Fortunately, I was attended to at Ultimate Electronics. I learned what I needed to about the different styles and then purchased the model that fit my needs. About a week later, I got a letter addressed to me with no return address. When I pulled out the small card inside the envelope and read it, I was pleasantly surprised. The Ultimate Electronic salesperson who helped me had sent a handwritten thank-you card to me thanking me for the recent purchase. Writing the card probably took the salesperson about two minutes, and the postage cost the company 32 cents. However, this is a very small fee to win over a current customer for a lifetime. The thank-you card helped me have a personal experience with the company. I felt the employees at Ultimate Electronics actually cared I had come into the business. Ultimately, they cared I had helped them stay in business.

Write Appreciation Messages

A note or letter expressing appreciation is always a treat and opportunities for these are almost unlimited. The format is less important than the tone of such a message. In fact, you can often be casual and creative in such messages as long as you project a pleasant tone. Handwritten notes can be as good as formally typed messages. Personal note paper can be used rather than letterhead. And, of course, such messages work great with internal customers.

To strengthen a note of appreciation,

1. *Mention or describe the specific actions, attitudes, or characteristics that you appreciate.* Just saying, "I appreciate you" is nice. But saying something more specific is likely to have more impact: "I appreciate the way you are open to new ideas" or "I appreciate your help in providing me with . . . .
2. *Use the person's name* in the body of the message. Don't overdo it, though—it may sound patronizing—but do personalize the message. Address readers as you would when talking to them. Use first names, nicknames, or more formal addresses, as appropriate. Don't call the reader "Bill" if you would normally call him "Mr. Kosinski."
3. *Do not send mixed strokes.* A goodwill message should be all positive. If you have negative information to convey, save it for a separate message. Do not say, "Tom, you did a really good job on the Wesson negotiations. I'm always proud to have you representing our company. But will you please quit wearing those loud ties? They made your appearance less than businesslike."
4. *Be conversational.* A goodwill letter should sound the way you would talk. Stuffiness or formality can damage the tone. Contractions ("I'm," "we'd," etc.) are fine. And even terms that are grammatically "incorrect" can create a pleasant tone ("Way-ta-go!" or "Attaboy!").

> It never hurts to spread a little goodwill. In doing so, be efficient yet personal.

The degree of formality you choose depends on what is comfortable for you. Some people prefer the more formal tone, but many enjoy a more conversational, breezy message.

Write Congratulations or Recognition Messages

Congratulation messages can follow the same guidelines as the appreciation note, although they may be slightly more formal. Be sure to:

1. *Mention the specific actions you are congratulating* the reader for (graduation from the company's advanced training program, promotion, bowling a 300 game, a son's advancement to Eagle Scout, etc.).

2. *Suggest that you understand some of the effort that went into the achievement.* "I know this reflects many hours of hard work."
3. *Express pride and support as appropriate.* "I'm proud to have worked with you and want you to know you'll have my continued support in your new position."

Express Sympathy or Condolences in Writing

Sooner or later we all face the experience of sharing grief. We are faced with the need to communicate with those who are dealing with the inevitable process of mourning. It is useful to understand something of the psychology of mourning.

Professor James Calvert Scott explains: "Mourning involves the psychological task of breaking the bonds with that which has been lost and eventually reinvesting that attachment in living people and things. Society's death-related rituals, including the letter of condolence, play a significant role in repairing and restoring the emotional and social damage caused by death."

Well-meaning family and friends often interfere with the grieving process by avoiding mention of the loss at the very time the bereaved need most to confront it. By doing so, they prevent the bereaved from experiencing the reality of death and the full range of emotions that are necessary in order to accomplish a healthy resolution. Working through grief is the process of consciously admitting and accepting the loss intellectually and emotionally. The ultimate goal of grief work is to be able to remember the loss without emotional pain and to direct emotions to the future.

The psychologically sound letter of condolence should help the bereaved to work through their grief. You can accomplish this by following these guidelines:

1. Acknowledge how you learned about and reacted to the death.
2. Avoid euphemisms relating to death and to the deceased person. Refer to him or her by name, not "the dearly departed"; say "died," not "expired."
3. Maintain a sincere, positive tone by focusing on the contributions of the deceased person. Perhaps relate a specific example of how he or she influenced your life.
4. Avoid quoting poetry, rhetorical writing, or Scripture unless you are certain that it will bring comfort. Your original thoughts are far more valued.
5. Make a specific offer of assistance, if possible. Offer to help with child care or to house visiting relatives, as appropriate. Anticipate your reader's needs and try to be of service.

APPLY A GENERAL PATTERN OF GOODWILL MESSAGES

A get-right-to-the-point approach usually works best in goodwill messages. Often the first words are "Thank you," "Congratulations," "I appreciate," or "I am sorry to hear . . . ."

The pattern, format, or even the grammar of a goodwill message is less important than the fact that it was sent and reflects a sense of caring. Typically a goodwill message takes only a few minutes to produce but offers a great return in improved relationships.

A manager friend of mine makes it a point to send short letters to the homes of employees whose work is exemplary. The payoff for such a simple action is that:

1. Employees know he recognizes and appreciates their good work.
2. By sending the message to the home, the employer enables the employee's family to share in the praise.
3. The letter becomes a part of the employee's personnel file and can be used when preparing a performance review.
4. By noting that copies have been sent to higher levels of management ("cc: The Boss"), employees know they are getting additional attention.

Opportunities for goodwill notes come up almost daily. Besides on-the-job performance, personal and family accomplishments can be acknowledged. A daughter's wedding, an impressive bowling score, and recognition for community service can all be opportunities to show you care.

If you can't think of a reason to send a note to customers or friends, perhaps you can clip a story or article out of a magazine that you know they are interested in. Send that with a brief note acknowledging that you are aware of their interest.

Create Goodwill for the Organization

The "public" form of a goodwill message may take the form of a press release. Here the intent is to convey good news or to shed light on some positive aspect of an organization via a message broadcast through print or electronic media. Although not personalized, such messages can help create a positive image for the company and attract customers.

Get Appropriate Publicity with News Releases

A properly produced news release can be the backbone of any publicity campaign or image-building effort. While sending out news releases is the most obvious part of getting mentioned in the media, creating real news about your product or service is actually the first step. The next step is identifying and contacting the appropriate media to receive your news release. To get the best results, send your news releases only to media whose audiences are very likely to be interested in what you have to say.

Follow up on any press releases you send to the media.

Follow-up often gets overlooked, but it is crucial to any publicity campaign. Make follow-up phone calls to the media contacts to make sure they received your release, but don't try to pressure them into running it. If they run it, be sure to thank them. If they don't run it, don't call and complain.

If you're certain your releases would be of interest to a certain medium's audience, keep sending them new information and following up. The more releases you send, the more likely one of them will eventually be run. Don't get discouraged, just keep trying. If your releases are newsworthy, with enough patience and persistence, you'll get them placed.

Write the News Release

The basic tool for generating publicity (i.e., public goodwill) is the news release. With it companies can get free publicity from newspapers, magazines, radio, and television. Most of the news in newspapers and magazines comes from news releases sent out by companies, government agencies, associations, and various individuals and groups.

News releases provide much of the information found in the media.

Since a properly prepared news release is the cornerstone of any publicity campaign, be sure that you create a good one. While some room for creativity exists, a common, easy-to-follow format is used for most successful news releases. It has several key elements: the originator (you), the release date, the contact, a headline, and the double-spaced copy itself.

If you send out the news release on your company stationery, that takes care of the originator. All you have to do is type NEWS or NEWS RELEASE in capital letters at the top of the letterhead.

The release date is the date you want the story released. In many cases, it can say "FOR IMMEDIATE RELEASE." This is probably best, unless there is some overriding reason why the story can't be released before a certain date. Also necessary are the name and telephone number of a person to contact for further information.

The headline should appear in capital letters, six spaces below the contact line. It should be as clever and catchy as possible so that it captures the attention and arouses the interest of the editor or producer. Newspaper headlines can be used as models of how to write news release headlines. Try for a headline that compels the reader to read the entire release.

Eight spaces below the headline, begin the body of the release. It should be double-spaced and written like a newspaper article, with the most important information in the first paragraph, the supporting information next, and the least important information last. A news release can be any length, but a one-page release is probably best. If you do use more than one page, place the word "MORE" at the bottom center of the first page.

You can use news releases to announce the start of your company, new products and services, speaking engagements, and appearances on radio or television shows, or any other event connected with your company that has potential news value.

Whom you address your news releases to is extremely important. Newspapers and magazines have specialized editors, while each radio and television talk show has a specific producer. Your best chance for getting the publicity you desire is to direct your release to the appropriate editor or producer.

Because your release may be reprinted verbatim in some newspapers or organizational newsletters, spend ample time to compose clever, readable releases. In some cases, your release may even be used as the basis for a feature story.

It's a good idea for your news releases to end with a "For more information" paragraph. Use this to give your company's name, address, and phone number and to offer a free brochure or some other kind of promotional material. Doing this encourages people to contact your business, giving you new prospects and an opportunity to gauge the relative impact of that particular coverage.

> A press release (or news release) can be a great way to inform customers and potential customers about the goings-on in your company.

A FINAL THOUGHT

Written communication is often overlooked as a customer service tool. Many people are uncomfortable writing, but by applying some simple techniques such as those discussed in this chapter, they can use the power of written messages to build customer relationships. To reapply comedian Woody Allen's comment, "Eighty percent of all success is just showing up," 80 percent of your success can come from simply using written messages for customer service. Don't be overly worried about the "correctness" of your writing; just write the way you'd talk and let the customer know that you care enough to send a written message.

Summary of Key Ideas

- Written messages are an often overlooked tool for creating customer satisfaction and loyalty.
- Goodwill notes are those you send even though you don't have to. Their power arises from customers' surprise at receiving them.
- Originality helps boost the power of goodwill messages. Almost everybody sends Christmas cards; be more creative and you'll get greater impact.
- Be direct and straightforward in routine messages. Get right to the point.
- Create goodwill via news releases about the organization.

Key Terms and Concepts

Appreciation messages
Congratulations or recognition messages
Follow-up letters
Goodwill
News release
Routine informative messages
Sympathy messages

Self-Test Questions

1. What are some important tips to apply when writing goodwill messages?
2. Name several situations when a sales follow-up letter would be appropriate.
3. What is a routine message? Give an example.
4. What are four important steps to writing an appreciation letter?
5. How can you better your chances of getting a news release published?

Application Activity: Prepare a Generic Customer Thank-You Note

Using the guidelines in this chapter, draft a thank-you note that could be used for immediate follow-up with your customers. (Use an imaginary business if you are not currently employed.) Leave blank spaces where others in your organization could fill in details as they use the same format for thank-you notes.

Application Activity: Prepare a Practice News Release

Using the guidelines in this section, write a brief news release from "You, Inc."

Announce a significant achievement or bit of information about you. (Don't worry too much about newsworthiness at this point. Our purpose is to practice the news release format.)

Foundation Skill

9

Understanding the One-to-One Customer Future[1]

Changing Conventions in Customer Service

Instead of centering on products and brands, [the] new form of business competition centers on customers and customer relationships—at the individual level.

—Don Peppers and Martha Rogers

WHAT YOU'LL LEARN IN THIS CHAPTER

- Certain kinds of paradigm shifts are transforming marketing and customer service.
- One-to-one marketing and personalized service are changing the face of commerce.
- Such technological changes are having an impact on people in all segments of society.
- Businesspeople need to know about relationship marketing and service.

The Way It Is

Back from the Future[2]

In late 1991, the telegraph industry's life was taken, suddenly and brutally, by the facsimile machine. For more than 150 years, the telegram stood for immediacy and importance. It was an icon for urgency. But now Western Union has closed down its telegraph service around the world. The fax was a new technology the telegram could not survive.

The shift from teletype and telegram to facsimile transmission represents one aspect of what some business consultants term a "paradigm shift"—a discontinuity in the otherwise steady march of business progress.

The automobile was another discontinuity, one that radically transformed both the economy and society. When the automobile first appeared, it seemed to be merely a horseless version of the well-known carriage. Predicting the consequences of the automobile's introduction would have been nearly impossible. Who would have imagined that a noisy, smelly, unreliable machine would eventually be responsible for the creation of suburbs, the fractionalization of families, and the growth of supermarkets, malls, and the interstate highway system?

Today we are passing through a technological discontinuity of epic proportions, and most of us are not even remotely prepared. The old paradigm—a system of mass production, mass media, and mass marketing—is being replaced by a totally new paradigm, a one-to-one economic system.

The one-to-one future will be characterized by customized production (sometimes called mass customization), individually addressable media, and one-to-one marketing, totally changing the rules of business competition and growth. Instead of market share, the goal of most business competition will be share of the customer—one customer at a time.

> Successful businesses of the future will focus not on market share as much as on share of the customer.

Having the size necessary to produce, advertise, and distribute vast quantities of standardized products won't be a precondition for success. Instead, products will be increasingly tailored to individual tastes, electronic media will be inexpensively addressed to individual consumers, and many products ordered over the phone will be delivered to the home in eight hours or less.

In the one-to-one future, businesses will focus on the kinds of profits that can be realized from long-term customer retention and lifetime values.

The discontinuity we are now living through will be every bit as disruptive to our lives, and as beneficial, as the Industrial Revolution was to the lives of our great-grandparents. The way we compete will change dramatically enough over just the next few years to alter the very structure of our society, empowering some and disenfranchising others.

It would be difficult to underestimate the cataclysmic changes that will jolt society as a result of this paradigm shift. It will disrupt everything, but ultimately one-to-one technology will create an entrepreneurial froth of opportunities. When the dust has settled, new businesses—millions of them—most not even conceived today, will have sprung up across the economic landscape as naturally and randomly as wild flowers after a severe winter.

In a world in which communication and information are practically free, the economic system will be driven more than ever before by genuine innovation and human creativity. In such a world, ideas will be the medium of exchange.[3]

In customer service, massive levels of communication on the Internet will greatly multiply the ripple effect problem we discussed in Chapter 1.

UNDERSTAND THE TECHNOLOGY SHIFTS FOR THE NEW FUTURE

The demise of the telegraph industry is, of course, only one of countless examples of so-called paradigm shifts—new ways of thinking about and doing business. The list of obsolete products and services replaced by new, previously unimagined ones is long. And the pace of these changes seems ever-increasing. Yet many of us forget today's commonplace devices that were not yet used as recently as 1980. For example, there were no automatic teller machines, laser printers, or cellular phones. But even more incredible, "the number of televisions with remote control devices was statistically insignificant. There were no compact disks, almost no videocassette recorders, and no video rental stores. Only restaurants had microwave ovens. Facsimile machines cost several thousand dollars each, took five minutes or more to transmit a single page, and were found only in very large companies. No one had a personal computer."[5]

Technology has changed our lives dramatically in the past few decades.

And we haven't even touched on the Internet, with its astronomical impact on commerce and customer relationships. Within a few years, e-commerce will account for trillions of dollars and will become commonplace throughout the world. Already the increase in products purchased via the Net doubles and triples each year. Whole books are addressing customer service in e-commerce. The following is from the preface to one such book, *Customer Service on the Internet,* by Jim Sterne:[6]

> Until recently, the computer's impact on business was measured almost exclusively in terms of speed and convenience. That is, a business kept working the way it always had, but it worked faster, and it worked with fewer people. In other words, many businesses have harnessed computers to become more competitive in operations. But continually declining information processing costs and rising computational power now mandate a transformation in the way businesses actually compete for customers.
>
> The astounding capabilities of the microchip have dramatically changed the business landscape—not just boosting the speed and reducing the cost of doing business, but changing the actual dimension of competition, too. Instead of centering on products and brands, this new form of business competition centers on customers and customer relationships—at the individual level.
>
> In essence, computers have now made it possible to create an individual "customer feedback loop," integrating the production and service delivery processes into the research and promotion processes. The customer database allows a business to tell its customers apart and remember them individually. With interactivity, customers can talk to businesses—businesses are no longer limited to talking at their customers. And, with mass customization technology more and more businesses can actually make and deliver a single, customized product or service—cost efficiently—to an individual customer.
>
> This feedback loop renders obsolete nearly every traditional marketing principle any business used to hold sacred. No longer is the marketer confined to dealing with awareness levels, or attitudes and brand preferences, or even competitive product comparisons. No longer must he project the results of sample surveys to a larger population.
>
> Instead, the customer and the business together are now redefining what it means to participate in a commercial relationship. It is becoming a collaborative, interactive world. The new dynamic of competition is based on doing battle for one customer at a time.
>
> There are many things a business should do to cope with this shift in the competitive ground. First and foremost, it should realize that its most valuable, most indispensable asset is not the product it sells, and not the service it renders. A business's only truly irreplaceable asset is the customer it serves, and the relationship it enjoys with that customer. Developing relationships with individual customers, differentiating one customer from the next, and treating each one as a separate, identifiable participant in the commercial relationship—these are the competitive activities of the most successful businesses today.

Second, a business should try to increase the level of interaction with its customers, across all media. If a business values its customers as its principal asset it will want to interact with those customers at every conceivable opportunity. Interactivity can occur in a wide variety of ways, from the touch-tone phone, to the ATM, to the cashier's station at the store, to the Internet.

Third, a business should be trying to customize whatever it can to the individually expressed needs of individual customers. This might mean tailoring a manufactured product, or it might simply mean invoicing a customer not on the seller's billing cycle but on the customer's paying cycle. The point is, in order to center the business around individual customers, the firm must learn to change its behavior with respect to the feedback it gets from each.

It's easy to find examples of technology that reflect huge changes in our way of life. But perhaps just as significant have been the social, economic, and political shifts that impact business, the professions, and customer satisfaction.

RECOGNIZE THE SOCIAL AND ECONOMIC SHIFTS FOR THE NEW FUTURE

Aside from technology, other noteworthy changes affect business and customer relationships today. On the social and economic scene we see substantial demographic shifts. Workforces are increasingly diverse—made up of people from a wide range of economic circumstances, cultures, and religions, and both genders. Today's workforce consists of more two-income families and single parents with the associated family responsibilities this poses. We have an increasingly educated workforce, and its people are less tolerant than ever of mindless, repetitive work. People expect today to be more involved in organizational decisions, to have their input considered.

All these people are, of course, customers. Their shifting social conditions have stimulated demand for new and different products and services. Working couples have come to value shopping efficiency and convenience. Ethnically diverse neighborhoods have caused restaurants serving many kinds of food to flourish. Fast food and take-home cuisine have become the mainstay of some busy families.

Politically, organizations face increasing government regulations, most of which reflect levels of social awareness not previously considered in the business world. Equal employment opportunities for people of all backgrounds, persons with disabilities, and both genders are among the more notable changes of recent years. Likewise, concern for the environment, employee health and safety, and even emotional well-being have become hallmarks of today's successful businesses. Caring companies attract and keep better employees (internal customers) and ultimately succeed in the marketplace. Most companies are aware of "green" issues: recycling and ecologically friendly packaging. In short, customers have come to expect different kinds of satisfaction.

Are you ready to grab onto the whirlwind of change and be a player in this exciting time of business and professional changes? Many people resist or even fear change of the kinds described. It demands that they learn new skills and adapt to new ways of meeting customer requirements. Consequently, many people are left behind. Will you be one of them?

USE THE NEW MEDIA FOR A ONE-TO-ONE FUTURE

Media changes have made big differences in the ways organizations communicate among their own members and with the world outside. In addition to the obvious speed and efficiency advantages of today's media, other considerations have an impact on customer relationships. One of the most significant trends is in the increasing ability to efficiently generate personalized, one-to-one messages tailored to the needs and wants of individuals, especially customers, coworkers, and associates.

> One-to-one, individually tailored messages can now be sent to huge audiences.

Communication experts have long recognized that (1) the more we know about our message receiver(s), and (2) the more we personalize a message to the receiver's wants and interests, the more effective we will be in communicating and building relationships.

The power of customized messages in business and professional communication should not be underestimated. In an organization's marketing function, for example, we are seeing a shift from mass marketing—sending the same messages to a massive number of people in hopes that some of them will respond favorably—to individualized marketing whereby we send a unique individualized message to each person. This personalization began with word processing, which gave us the ability to produce "merged" letters that include personalized sections interspersed with the generic message.

> Today's media go beyond the simple merging of names and addresses.

Today, mass mailers routinely take advantage of this ability to personalize sales letters, sweepstakes entry forms, and even the envelopes they are sent in. But today's media let us go far beyond what has been done, to now include past buying information and personal preferences to convey a sense that we know and understand our reader.

With the help of technology, we are progressively moving toward one-to-one marketing that can create long-term *relationships* with customers and provide for a wide range of their needs. With mass marketing and its communication media, such as mass media ads or junk mail, the goal has been to gain a larger *share of the market.* If, for example, your store accounts for 10 percent of all the menswear sold in your town, mass marketing tries to get that up to 12 or 15 percent. The assumption is, of course, that a larger share of the market means more profits. Unfortunately, this is becoming less of a sure thing. Advertising costs have increased and results have dropped. It costs more and more money to get a new customer into your business using traditional approaches.

One-to-one marketing builds relationships that allow businesses to earn a larger share of the customer's business.

The one-to-one marketing instead focuses on establishing an ongoing relationship with existing customers. You do this by gathering as much information about them as possible and responding to their needs. A menswear store today may do very little mass advertising and still be very profitable by keeping close to its customers and meeting all their clothing needs. A bank or credit union may expand its services to eventually handle all its customers' financial needs. This is called getting a larger *share of the customer* and has been found to be very profitable.

Interactivity Options Now Available

Today's technology makes the one-to-one process possible. In the past, keeping track of customer names and addresses, sales data, and personal preferences was a complex and time-consuming process. Many people have kept such customer data on 3×5-inch cards in a file box. As the number of customers grew, the task became impractical. Today's computers and point-of-sale electronic data gathering devices, however, make it easy. We can now track individual preferences, poll customers about their needs, and customize services and products to meet those needs. Many stores are now offering discount coupons to the customer at the checkout counter. If the customer buys a six-pack of Pepsi, the scanner generates a coupon for 50 cents off on Frito-Lay potato chips. (Frito-Lay is a division of PepsiCo.) People can also get coupons for only the products they buy on the Net.

Interactivity between a business and its customers now lets consumers instantly respond to advertisements through their TV sets and computers. This technology has advertisers "scurrying around looking for opportunities to experiment," according to marketing executives. There is a huge future in interactive advertising, "only no one knows when the future starts," says Irving A. Miller of Toyota Motor Sales USA.[7] I'll talk more about cyberspace and interactive buying later in this chapter.

All Is Ultimately One-to-One

The one-to-one principle holds for internal customer relationships too. By keeping closely attuned to their employees' preferences, talents, and wants, managers build long-term relationships that can be mutually beneficial to the company. A fully utilized employee is the counterpart to the fully served customer.

On the social, friendship level, knowing about and addressing the interests, needs, and wants of friends has always been a major factor in building rapport and lifelong relationships. Interactivity—the two way flow of information—is the key.

> Interactivity is the key to effective relationship building.

Many effective "networkers" keep reminder data on friends and acquaintances. We know a highly successful business entrepreneur who, from the earliest days of his career, kept an index card on each person he met. On the card he would jot notes about the person's family, interests, pets, birthdates and anniversaries, accomplishments—even favorite jokes. Then, each time he spoke on the phone, he'd pull out the person's card and use ideas from it in the conversation. That's one-to-one communication. And today's media magnify this ability.

USE MEDIA BREAKTHROUGHS TO ALLOW MORE ONE-TO-ONE COMMUNICATION

Today's communication media typically combine the power of computers to allow such one-to-one relationship building on a larger scale. These media have the following characteristics:

1. They are *individually addressable and highly adaptive* to unique needs. They permit messages to be fully tailored to each customer, not just superficially modified versions of a form letter.
2. They are *interactive,* creating two-way, not one-way, communication. They make it easy for customers to give their feedback and reactions to messages.
3. They are *affordable and powerful.*

Are such media available to the typical businessperson or professional? More than any time in history, the answer is an unqualified yes. Even the smallest business or individual proprietorship can afford much of today's technology. We are steadily moving toward more effective one-to-one service in business and the professions, supported by electronic media that can individualize messages.

UNDERSTAND THAT SOME THINGS REMAIN THE SAME

Having said all we have about technological, economic, social, and organizational change, we must also acknowledge that many aspects of the customer satisfaction process remain the same. In particular, psychological and behavioral factors have changed little. Human and organizational needs remain largely the same. A basic sense of caring, concern, and competence will continue to play a critical role in building customer satisfaction and loyalty. In fact, for some, the advent of so much technology has rekindled a hunger for the old-fashioned human touch. That is one reason The Gap clothing stores (among others) display products on large tables that become easily messed up. Rearranging the table gives the clerks something to do and keeps them nearby to interact with customers.

CHANGE THE OLD CONVENTIONS

You probably have heard someone describe a super salesperson as one who can sell anything to anyone—even ice cubes in Alaska. The old convention taught that dynamic sales skills are the ticket to success. If the salesperson could give a decent presentation of the product and slam the consumer with an amazing close, then the consumer would buy. That was it. Transaction complete.

In our day, a new convention is on the rise. Although presentation and closing are still important to the sales process, an even more vital element supersedes both of these—the customer's satisfaction. Today's consumers face an unprecedented number of choices. Because of our free enterprise system, consumers have hundreds of places to go to buy the very same product. What makes the customer choose which place of business to buy from? Are choices based on quality, price, and convenience, or on customer service? How do you decide where to buy clothes, groceries, automobiles, electronics, and other consumer goods? What is most important to you as a consumer? There is no mystery in the answers to these questions. A consumer goes where the most is offered—the most value, the most efficient systems, and the most pleasant and personable transactions. It is that simple.

APPLY RELATIONSHIP MARKETING: THE ONLY WAY TO SURVIVE IN THE FUTURE

> Customers in a free-market economy expect good products at reasonable cost. This is a given. What they don't always expect is great service.

Companies may argue they have the best quality product at great prices. The fact is, customers have gotten used to having quality products at good prices. These things are givens. They alone cannot readily distinguish one business from the competition.

But customers don't yet expect great service. They continue to expect less than marginal service. Why? Because that is what they've been getting in the past. Can you see the enormous opportunity that exists for building a strong competitive advantage through excellent E-Plus service?

Think back to when you were a child. Do you remember a corner grocer or a candy store manager? Did he know who you were or who your parents were? A typical comment from the grocer might have been, "Hi Billy, it's good to see you. Did you have a good vacation to the Grand Canyon?" Or from the candy store manager, "Hello Susie, last time you were here you bought a half-pound of licorice. Can I get you the same thing, or would you like to try something different?" This is relationship marketing—having a one-to-one relationship with your customers. Every company—from a Fortune 500 to a local babysitter—can utilize relationship marketing with just a bit of training. In fact, relationship marketing is limited only by the creativity of the people in the company.

> Relationship marketing opportunities are limited only by one's imagination.

With the use of creativity, the opportunity to exceed customers' expectations extends well beyond just calling someone by name. That is a great start, but consider the following example given by Michael Gerber in his book, *The E Myth Revisited,* to see how far superior service can be taken:

On his way back to his home in San Francisco from a business trip, Michael decided to stop for the night in a little hotel overlooking the Pacific. When he arrived at the reception desk, a well-dressed woman quickly appeared and welcomed him to the hotel. Within three minutes from the greeting, he was ushered into his room by the bellboy. The room was decorated with plush carpeting, white-on-white bedding, natural cedar walls, and a stone fireplace. The fireplace grate had oak logs, rolled paper, and matches waiting to be used.

After changing in his room, Michael walked to the restaurant. The hotel receptionist had made him reservations for the restaurant at the time of his check-in. Michael was immediately shown to his table upon arrival—even though others without reservations were waiting. When he got back to his room that night, the pillows were plumped up, the bed was turned down and there was a fire blazing in the fireplace. On the nightstand was a glass of brandy and a card that read, "Welcome to your first stay at Venetia. I hope it has been enjoyable. If there is anything I can do for you, day or night, please don't hesitate to call. Kathi."

In the morning Michael woke up to the smell of coffee. When he went into the bathroom he found a perking coffee pot. A card by the pot read, "Your brand of coffee. Enjoy! K." Michael had been asked the night before at the restaurant which brand of coffee he preferred. Now it was bubbling in his room. Michael heard a polite knock on the door. When he opened the door, he saw the *New York Times* lying on the mat. When Michael had checked in, the reservationist had asked him what paper he preferred. Now his preferred paper was at his room for him to read.

Michael explains the service at the hotel has been exactly the same every time he has gone back. But after the first visit, he was never asked his preferences again.[8]

This is a great example of relationship marketing and of customer service. By "learning" his preferences, the hotel management was able to manipulate a common experience into one that was very personal for Michael—exceeding any expectations he might have had. To be successful relationship marketers, you must become personal with your customers. After having a personalized experience with a business, a customer becomes very loyal. Think about it—would you patronize another hotel in the area after having a similar experience? Why would anyone want to take the chance of getting the "expected" service of any other hotel? You can begin to see why relationship marketing is so powerful and so correlated with customer service.

GAIN CUSTOMER SHARE, NOT MARKET SHARE

Let's talk once again about the important concept of customer share. Progressive companies are coming to see the wisdom of focusing on share of customers rather than share of market.[9] Consider the following two competing flower businesses:

- The owners of flower Company A have worked very hard, with a mass-marketing focus, in order to get a good piece of the market. They calculated that Company A has about 20 percent market share. In other words, for every dollar spent on flowers in the market, Company A gets 20 cents.
- The owners of flower Company B, on the other hand, have worked very hard to gain a relationship with every one of the top purchasers of flowers (those who buy flowers on the most consistent basis). They estimate that they have a 20 percent customer share. That is, for every ten customers who buy flowers, two of them buy flowers from Company B 100 percent of the time.

Which company is better off in the long run? Remember who Company B focused on: the customers who are frequent buyers—the top customers of the industry. Therefore, Company B enjoys much greater efficiency in its marketing—its customers are the best customers to have. They know them and they massaged their relationship to gain even more of their flower business. They win.

If a company can win over the top customers, then its chance of survival is much better than just having a percentage of the market. Managers need to think of the present value of a customer's future business. An example illustrates what I mean: In the book, *Customers for Life,* Carl Sewell explains the importance of thinking about the present value of future business.[10] Carl owns one of the largest luxury car dealerships in the country. He has calculated that every customer has the potential of bringing his dealership $332,000 in sales. If an average car costs about $25,000, and if people buy on average 12 cars, then the total sale is $300,000. Add service and parts and each customer of Carl's dealership is worth about $332,000 in sales.

Mark Grainer, chairman of the Technical Assistance Research Programs Institute (TARP), similarly estimates that a loyal supermarket customer is worth $3,800 annually.[11] Over the course of a lifetime, this could easily add up to more than $150,000 in sales. Furthermore, a businessperson who frequently flies to different parts of the world could easily spend over $50,000 annually on air travel. This customer could be worth over $1 million in revenue for an airline! This is what we mean by the present value of future business.

> The present value of future business is an estimate of the total a customer would potentially spend with you.

With this kind of long-range dollar thinking, who wouldn't give priority to customer share rather than market share? The customer you already have is infinitely more likely to buy from you again, while ever scrambling for new customers drains your marketing budget and energy. Remember, though, the only way to increase customer share is to build a relationship with your customer and to enhance your customer's satisfaction and loyalty.

TRY DATABASE MARKETING: AN INTEGRAL PART OF FUTURE CUSTOMER SERVICE

Every day thousands of inventions are registered. Occasionally, one of these inventions changes the way businesses do things forever. Just 20 years ago, most businesses were without personal computers. In our day, however, computers have become a common "must-have" for every type of business.

Because of computers, we are able to store great amounts of detailed information and retrieve any of this information in just seconds. The computer has greatly enhanced the possibilities for any company to begin relationship marketing and increase customer service. When managers collect information, they put the information into a database. This database can be accessed in the future to retrieve any of this information.

> Databases of customer information are invaluable in building business relationships.

Successful businesspeople have always used databases—the ones in their heads. Remember the corner grocer and the candy store manager? They knew most of their customers' names, and they probably even knew what each customer purchased the last time he or she was in the store. They stored this kind of information in their minds—the most important database. When businesses began to get larger, managers started writing pertinent information down. This information would be filed away and located at a later time. Today, most companies input this information into computer databases. The database saves space, time, and, over the long run, money. That is what computers do best: remember things.

An increasingly popular use of a computer database can be seen at stores that invite shoppers to join a "club" that gives them better prices in exchange for data. The customer may be given a key chain bar code that is scanned each time the shopper buys. The data then develops a profile of that customer and his or her buying patterns.

With the use of such databases, managers can know exactly when and how many times you went to their store. They know what you bought on each visit and the items you are most interested in. This information is extremely valuable and can be used for various purposes. It can personalize your shopping profile so that a clerk might be electronically reminded of a purchase you made earlier and can ask how that merchandise is working for you. For example, when you go to the checkout stand at a sophisticated electronics store, the employee can immediately get your information, call you by name, and ask, "Has the CD player you bought two weeks ago been working well for you?"

With the database of information, the managers can also market directly to those who would benefit most from the marketing. For instance, suppose the managers have received word from Hewlett-Packard that a $5 customer rebate will be given for each Hewlett-Packard ink cartridge sold. An office supply store can then send a mailing to anyone who has bought a Hewlett-Packard printer or Hewlett-Packard printer supplies within the last five years. With this information, the store can market to individuals—in other words, utilize relationship marketing. The customers see this as great customer service—they only get the coupons and ads they, personally, are interested in.

Think how you could E-Plus even these techniques. For example, a gift catalog company, using its database, implemented a new program that can:[12]

1. Send any number of gifts to your friends and relatives when you order them from the catalog up to 15 months in advance.
2. Deliver the gift on the day specified on the order form. The customer will never again miss any important date.

Service Snapshot

The Reminder

Thanks to computer databases, Fischer Florist in Atlantic City, New Jersey is able to collect information and use it for retention of customers.[13] Every day the managers at Fischer Florist send out reminder cards to certain customers. A reminder card might read as follows:

> Dear Mr. Jones: On March 29, last year, you remembered Jenny's birthday by sending her one dozen roses. Enclosed is a catalog of other beautiful flowers we offer. Please call our toll-free telephone number to place an order. We will make sure Jenny has your choice of flowers on that special day. Thank you for your business. We look forward to hearing from you.

When Mr. Jones calls, he must only tell the flower shop what flowers to send. Jenny's address, telephone number, and available times for delivery are already in the computer database. Likewise, Mr. Jones' credit card number is on file and can easily be confirmed and used.

3. Bill the customer's credit card only when the gifts are sent. Send an invoice to the customer for each gift charged to the account within five working days.
4. Send a reminder postcard to the customer before the gift is sent out, explaining whom the gift is going to and what the gift is.
5. Send all customers an updated catalog periodically. This new catalog has all the previous years' names preprinted on the order sheet, and the customer can add any new names to the bottom.
6. Provide a 24-hour toll-free telephone number for any changes or updates the customer might have.

With the use of a database, the information needed to do all this is stored easily, and the catalog store employees most likely have less work than they did before the service was implemented. Best of all, the managers can see almost exactly their sales revenue for the near future, thus helping financial planning for the company.

To add an interactive dimension to this service, the company includes two short questions on the customer order form. They ask the customers, What would you like to see our catalog service include in the future? and, What are some additional products you would like us to have in our gift catalog? Bingo! Customer preferences and expectations are revealed and E-Plus opportunities become clear.

USE CONTACT MANAGEMENT SYSTEMS

Contact management is the process of managing, tracking, and organizing contacts with your customers and potential customers. Physicians are professionals who are expected to do a good job at recording information about any patient visit. Many doctors dictate the information on a tape recorder and then have a secretary type the record later. This is a form of contact management. But it's not just for physicians any more. Imagine the following scenario:

> You walk into work one morning. Your secretary tells you one of your customers, John, is on the phone. John wants to know if the delivery time of two weeks is still possible. John also forgot the prices and quantities you had quoted him and would like to get them now before he goes into his meeting in five minutes. "Wow," you think to yourself, "which customer is John anyway?" Finally, you find the two different files John's information is in and you pick up the phone to call him back. Just then a customer walks into your office and says to you, "Where were you? You were supposed to come to my office and present your product to the Board of Trustees this morning. I'm sorry but I don't think you will be good enough to get the contract."

With better contact management, the unfortunate scenario can be resolved. The idea of contact management is to record every important detail of any communication with the customer. This information may include price quotes, dates of last contacts, dates of future meetings, promises made, reminders of any special information, letters or advertisements sent, and so on. This information must be organized and filed in such a way that it is readily available. Today, companies are using computerized contact management software to do this.

The software allows you to file away great amounts of information that can be brought up in seconds. For example, if the phone rings and John is on the phone, you can open any file with the name John and see exactly who he is, what you have promised him, when you are supposed to contact him next, and what you should be talking to him about. Most software programs allow you to search all customers for general information as well. For example, if you like to be proactive and contact your customers on a regular basis, contact management software can search for customers who have not been called for at least two weeks.

> Contact management software can be of tremendous value to virtually any business.

Because you can readily access information about your customer, you can build a stronger relationship. For instance, if a customer mentions that she is going out to dinner (say, at Chuck E Cheese) for her daughter's birthday, you can add a note in your contact management software. The next time you talk with this customer, you can ask, "How was your daughter's birthday dinner?" Questions like this get a customer thinking about you as a concerned friend, not just another person trying to sell her something.

Although large companies may use highly specialized, custom contact management software, most of us can use software that is sold at any local software store. There is no reason for a small company to spend thousands of dollars having contact manager software or database software custom made. Action Plus, Sales Ally, Bizbase Gold, Maximizer, and ACT 2.0 are all good contact managers that suit the needs of most businesses and only cost between $70 and $500.

Service Snapshot

Special Service for Best Customers

Hertz Car Rental knew they had problems when people were getting upset about having to wait in long lines to get their rental cars. Many businesspeople travel on very tight schedules and need to have a car quickly. Hertz knew that, unless some action was taken quickly, they would lose many of their most valuable and frequent renters. Hertz launched a special service—the #1 Gold Club—for those who needed their rental cars quickly. The #1 Gold Club members can call ahead of time to reserve a car. When members get off the plane, a shuttle is waiting for them at the curb to take them to the car. The shuttle driver can welcome them by name and explain that the shuttle trip is just two minutes. The shuttle drops the customer off at the reserved car. The engine is running, the trunk lid is open, and today's issue of the *Wall Street Journal* is on the front seat. Members get in the car and drive to the gate, where they show their driver's license and #1 Gold Card. No lines. No hassle.

TAP INTO THE ELECTRONIC FUTURE

Predicting the future in an ever-changing world is, of course, impossible. However, we can be sure to expect some application of new technologies like these:

Internet Shopping

Companies of all sizes and shapes are scrambling to get a home page and dive into e-commerce. A user of the Internet from anywhere in the world can dial up a home page and receive product information, prices, instructions, and even coupons. Soon, we can count on virtually every business marketing on the Internet. Internet access is regularly used in about a third of the homes in America as of this writing and is growing fast. Very soon it will be as common as the telephone.

Virtual Reality (VR) Shopping

Another use of technology is growing just behind today's Net shopping. Imagine yourself at your home and the weekly chore of grocery shopping has come again. You walk over to your computer, dial up the local grocery store, and start perusing the aisles—just as if you were there. In VR you see the grocery aisles and can maneuver your "virtual" self down the aisles. No traffic. No carts to bump into. Just you with free run of the grocery store. With your VR joystick, you reach out and put the groceries you would like into your virtual basket. When you are done with your shopping, you reach out with your virtual arm and touch the sign that says Done. Within an hour the groceries are delivered to your home.

Can you imagine the customer service opportunities companies will have with this technology? With just the use of computer programs, stores could individualize every aspect according to the customer's preferences. Let's take our example a bit further. While you are shopping in the VR store, you decide you would like to buy a six-pack of Pepsi. This time, instead of getting a Frito-Lay coupon, you see Greg, the "Virtual" Coca-Cola stocker. He hands you a 50¢-off coupon for a six-pack of Coca-Cola. All you need to do if you would like to automatically switch brands and save 50 cents is reach out and take the VR coupon. That'll tick off the Pepsi people, but it's an example of the increasing competitiveness in our VR world.

Imagine one more use of VR. You are interested in moving to California. You sit down at your computer and do a search for companies that build houses in California. You find a company and e-mail them some features you're looking for in a home. Within hours you go back to their site on the Internet, and take a virtual walk through the exact home you ordered. If you don't like it, you make some changes. When your house is exactly as you like it, you start taking virtual tours of locations for your home. Finally, you order your custom-designed house that you have seen—but that does not exist yet!

Interactive TV

Another important technological change will be in television. Right now consumers are forced to watch what they want to watch at certain times. Soon we can expect interactive television. If you want to watch an episode of *60 Minutes,* you will be able to order it and watch it at your convenience. You will have the option to watch shows free of charge with commercials or for a very small fee without commercials. Since advertisements on television shows today generate about 25¢ in revenue per watcher per show, some experts predict the cost of watching a show would be just 25¢ or so.

Interactive television offers much more than convenience in watching television shows. Everyone with a video camera will ultimately have the opportunity to get into viewers' homes. Just as anyone now can have a home page on the Internet, anyone in the future will be able to have a television show or television commercial. As consumers, we will dial up these commercials when we need a specific product or service. For example, if you're looking for a new car, you would just have to search the database for video information on vehicles. You will be able to watch information from BMW, GM, Ford, Acura, and from all other automobile companies. You will also be able to get video information about Sally down the street who is selling her 1996 red BMW 325i convertible.

With interactive television, the consumers will be in control of the information they receive. The broadcaster will just make the information available. Similarly, there will be no more junk mail, no more unwanted advertisements coming into the consumer's home. Consumers will select only the companies they want to get information from—ultimately they will decide which company to start a relationship with.

These are just a few of the examples of what the future holds. Few people doubt that the future will dramatically change the way we do business forever.

A FINAL THOUGHT

The future looks exciting for businesses, but most companies will need to make some major changes to be competitive—or they may decide to keep doing things the old-fashioned, down-home way they do now. That's an alternative strategy that may appeal to people who don't much care for all this newfangled stuff.

Some customers are concerned about privacy and the potential for intrusion into personal lives. For example, a recent promotion offered free computers to people as long as the company can gather infinite data about every click of the mouse made on that computer. In a sense, you would be selling your privacy for the price of a PC. Some customers might resist some of the techniques we've discussed but would be open to friendly, informal personalization found in local, neighborhood stores or shops.

Whatever strategy is employed, from highly sophisticated intelligent system databases to keeping mental notes on customer behaviors and preferences, one-to-one customer service and relationship building must stand as its cornerstone.

Summary of Key Ideas

- Today's business world is experiencing some important paradigm shifts in the direction of increased personalization of products and services.
- Because of advances in technology, one-to-one marketing and customer service will become the standard for businesses in the coming years.
- Other changes will continue to arise from social and economic shifts, media choice expansion, and increasing interactivity.
- Ultimately, much customer service success will stem from the ability to use relationship marketing to gain a greater share of the customer rather than just share of the market.
- Database marketing and contact management systems permit people to reach the most appropriate customers and build relationships with them.
- Electronic technologies like Internet shopping and virtual reality shopping will call for new creativity in designing and managing customer service.

Key Terms and Concepts

Contact management systems
Customer share versus market share
Interactive TV
Interactivity options
Internet shopping
One-to-one business
Paradigms
Present value of future business
Relationship marketing
Virtual reality shopping

Self-Test Questions

1. What kinds of paradigm shifts are transforming marketing and customer service?
2. What is one-to-one marketing? Give examples.
3. What is the difference between gaining a larger share of the market and a larger share of the customer?
4. What are some characteristics of today's one-to-one communication media?
5. What is relationship marketing and how can it best be used?
6. How can a company use database marketing to improve customer service?
7. What is a contact management system? How can it be used to boost customer satisfaction?

Activity: Scoping Out the One-to-One Future

1. Our opening story talks of "discontinuity" or "paradigm shifts" that literally change the world. List three discontinuities you are aware of

other than electronic technology. For each, describe three or more major changes that have resulted.

2. Among the most important determinants of customer satisfaction is the availability of feedback. Describe five ways organizations and individuals can increase their capabilities for gathering useful feedback.
3. Describe one or more examples of how businesses you know are using one-to-one communication to build a stronger relationship with you. (Note: Often these are little things done to build rapport and loyalty.)

NOTES

[1]The author acknowledges with appreciation the work of Clayton Eric Farr in developing an early draft of the part of this chapter dealing with the one-to-one future. Eric is a graduate of Brigham Young University and is completing his MBA at The Wharton School, University of Pennsylvania.

[2]Some of this material was adapted from P. Timm and J. Stead, *Communication Skills for Business and Professions* (Upper Saddle River, NJ: Prentice Hall, 1996), Chapter 1.

[3]Excerpted from D. Pepper and M. Rogers, *The One-to-One Future* (New York: Currency-Doubleday, 1993), pp. 3–6. Reprinted with permission.

[4]Jim Sterne, *Customer Service on the Internet: Building Relationships, Increasing Loyalty, and Staying Competitive* (New York: John Wiley & Sons, Inc., 1996), p. xxi.

[5]Pepper and Rogers, p. 14.

[6]Sterne, pp. vii–xviii.

[7]Quoted in G. P. Zachary, "Advertisers Anticipate Interactive Media as Ingenious Means to Court Customers," *Wall Street Journal,* August 17, 1994, p. B1.

[8]M. E. Gerber, *The E Myth Revisited* (New York: HarperCollins Publishers, Inc., 1995), pp. 188–192.

[9]Peppers and Rogers, pp. 18–51.

[10]C. Sewell and P. B. Brown, *Customers for Life* (New York: Pocket Books, 1990), p. 162.

[11]Peppers and Rogers, pp. 37–38.

[12]Peppers and Rogers, pp. 39–40.

[13]J. Griffin, *Customer Loyalty: How to Earn It; How to Keep It* (New York: Lexington Books, 1995), p. 125.

Appendix

How to Lead or Participate in an E-Plus Idea-Generating Meeting

Use the Group Process to Boost Customer Satisfaction and Loyalty

In this appendix we focus on 12 specific tips that enable you to conduct or participate in meetings designed to generate E-Plus ideas. When focused on improved service, such meetings can tap the ideas of the group to provide a gold mine of profitable customer service ideas.

ACTION TIP 1: MAKE THE MEETING'S PURPOSE ABSOLUTELY CLEAR

Meetings are of two general types: informational and problem solving. Don't confuse them. The most legitimate use of the group process is to elicit a variety of inputs on a specific problem or decision. E-Plus idea generation requires good group skills. Don't waste time at the meeting just giving out information.

Clarify the specific topic up front so that people come to the meeting with the right mind-set. Tell participants that the meeting will seek to generate E-Plus ideas from the VISPAC categories.

ACTION TIP 2: INVITE THE RIGHT PEOPLE

People invited to a meeting should:

1. *Have some expertise.* Typically customer contact people have the most experience with E-Plus opportunities, but others may also have ideas.
2. *Have a vested interest in the outcome of the discussion.* They want to improve customer loyalty.

3. *Have some skills in group decision making and be able to express themselves reasonably well.* Avoid the narrowminded, inflexible person.
4. *Share the overall values of the organization.* If participants are antagonistic or in disagreement with the company's goals, it makes no sense to have them participate in decisions affecting those goals.

Be sure, too, to invite the right *number* of people. Have enough to represent a variety of opinions but not so many that the process bogs down. E-Plus meetings work best with 4 to 12 participants.

ACTION TIP 3: ASSIGN ADVANCE PREPARATION

Participants should know what the meeting is about and what kinds of information or ideas they may need to gather and bring with them. If the central focus of the meeting is on generating E-Plus ideas to enhance customer *convenience,* telling people in advance lets them think about competitors' tactics, creative ideas being used by other companies, and perhaps needed data such as sales results others have experienced. Get people thinking on the right wavelength even before the meeting.

ACTION TIP 4: START ON TIME AND USE A REALISTIC SCHEDULE

A major objection of meeting attendees is the failure to start and end on time. Don't wait "a few minutes until the rest of the folks get here" or you'll find yourself doing so every time. Get a reputation for prompt starts and people will get there on time. Likewise, don't run overtime. If you've scheduled 90 minutes, stop at or before that deadline. If you really want to shock people, end the meeting early! When the work is done, quit.

Schedule breaks. Have refreshments. Encourage people to walk around the room. Do whatever is necessary to make the experience pleasant and satisfying.

ACTION TIP 5: CREATE A POSITIVE CLIMATE

If you are the leader, thank people for coming to the meeting. Let people know that they were selected because they can contribute valuable insights and ideas. A good psychological climate is best set by example. Let people know that the discussion can be casual and that they are encouraged to be creative.

Also, set up the meeting room appropriately so that participants:

1. Can see each other face to face (do not sit in rows, auditorium style).
2. Are provided with writing materials and table(s) to write on.
3. Use a chalkboard, newsprint flip charts, or transparencies to capture ideas.
4. Are encouraged to move around the room freely to relieve tension or fatigue.
5. Are provided with refreshments if the meeting will run more than a few hours.

ACTION TIP 6: BE AWARE OF THE "HIDDEN AGENDA"

Although we may agree on the discussion topic, people in meetings often have unspoken objectives—the so-called "hidden agenda." These may include such things as:

- Getting some "exposure" (i.e., to favorably impress others).
- Providing a "status arena" where they can assert power or show off their ability.
- Providing a chance to socialize with others.
- Diffusing decision responsibility so that one person won't have to take all the heat if a decision fails.
- Getting away from unpleasant work duties.

When achieving one's hidden agenda doesn't take away from the effectiveness of the group, don't worry about it. If the ulterior motives of the hidden agenda deter the group from accomplishing its work, talk with participants candidly (perhaps in private) and solicit their cooperation in putting the group's needs above their own.

ACTION TIP 7: REWARD GROUP MEMBER INPUT

Never let a group member's input be met with silence. To do so quickly extinguishes further input from that person—and others. Bear in mind that stating an opinion or idea can be somewhat risky for people. They might perceive a risk of being wrong, naive, unimaginative, or any of dozens of other possibilities.

By acknowledging contributions, we create a climate in which more will be offered. A simple "Good thought" or "You might be on to something there" can go a long way toward drawing further input. Even if the suggestion doesn't make much sense to you, you can come up with a neutral response like "Okay" or "Thanks."

ACTION TIP 8: MONITOR PRESSURES TO CENSOR

The problem of pressures to censor information is a bit more complex. Two common forms of such pressure are:

- individual dominance and
- groupthink.

Individual Dominance

In many groups, certain individuals dominate a discussion by force of their personality, organizational position, or personal status. These people may be particularly charming (and thus disproportionately influential because everybody likes them!) or highly autocratic or hardheaded. Reduce this dominance by drawing other people into the discussion.

Groupthink

Groupthink is a condition of like-mindedness that can arise in particularly cohesive groups. While cohesiveness is normally a good condition in groups, it can be carried too far. This can happen when the group members' desire for consensus or harmony becomes stronger than their desire for the best possible decision. Here are seven symptoms of groupthink:

1. An overemphasis on team play and getting along harmoniously.
2. A "shared stereotype" view that competitors or those in opposition to us are inept, incompetent, and incapable of doing anything well.
3. Self-censorship of group members; personal doubts are suppressed to avoid rocking the group's boat.
4. Rationalization to comfort one another and reduce any doubts regarding the group's agreed-on plan.
5. Self-appointed "mindguards" that function to prevent anyone from undermining the group's apparent unanimity and that "protect" the group from information that differs from their beliefs.
6. Direct pressure on those who express disagreement.
7. An expression of self-righteousness that leads members to believe their actions are moral or ethical, thus letting them disregard objections to their behavior.

Each of these symptoms of groupthink damages creative or original thinking and effective decisions.

ACTION TIP 9: DON'T ALLOW CONFLICT TO BECOME DESTRUCTIVE

Traditionally, it has been assumed that conflict should be avoided in meetings. The term conjures up images of fistfights or people screaming at each other. In reality, conflict is simply a state of incompatibility. It is neither good nor bad. What creates problems are the participants' reactions to it.

We typically respond to conflict in one of several ways:

1. We can attempt to *avoid* conflict by not expressing opposing views and by withholding any disagreement. Here we keep from rocking the boat and minimize the possibility of being subjected to rejection or reprisals from others. (Groupthinkers respond this way.) The drawback is that some good ideas—ideas that can best solve the group's problems—may be withheld.
2. We get into a *win–lose orientation,* leading to a no-holds-barred, open warfare among participants.
3. We *manage conflict* to regulate it but not eliminate confrontation. Recognizing that the abrasive actions of opposing views—like sandpaper on wood—polish the final product, skillful leaders seek free exchange of information but without the win–lose destructiveness of unregulated conflict. Accomplishing this calls for communication skills that encourage the generation of information without inhibiting or turning off participants.

The third response, managing conflict, is by far the most useful. Incidentally, a sense of humor helps. Mark McCormack said that, "Laughter is the most potent, constructive force for defusing business tension. Humor is what brings back perspective."

ACTION TIP 10: AVOID OVERCENTRALIZED LEADERSHIP

Effective meeting managers work to move the group away from the traditional leader toward group-centered leadership or self-managed teams. The leadership process of guiding and directing the group's activity should move from person to person within the group rather than be centered in one individual. Having each group member take some leadership role can overcome dominance and conflict problems. The result is what is called "group-centered leadership." This is contrasted with traditional leadership:

Traditional Leadership	***Group-Centered Leadership***
1. The leader directs, controls, polices the members, and leads them to the proper decision. Basically it is his or her group, and the leader's authority and responsibility are acknowledged by members.	1. The group, or meeting, is *owned* by the members, including the leader. All members, with the leader's assistance, contribute to its effectiveness.
2. The leader focuses attention on the task to be accomplished, brings the group back from any diverse wandering, and performs all the functions needed to arrive at the proper decision.	2. The group is responsible, with occasional and appropriate help from the leader, for reaching a decision that includes the participation of all and is the product of all.
3. The leader sets limits and uses rules of order to keep the discussion within strict limits set by the agenda. Her or she controls the time spent on each item lest the group wander fruitlessly.	3. Members of the group take responsibility for its task productivity, its methods of working, its assignments of tasks, and its plan for the use of the time available.
4. The leader believes that emotions are disruptive to objective, logical thinking, and should be discouraged or suppressed.	4. Feelings, emotions, and conflict are recognized by the members and the leader as legitimate factors in the discussion process.
5. The leader believes that a member's disruptive behavior should be handled by talking to the offender away from the group; it is the leader's task to do so.	5. The leader believes that any problem in the group must be faced and solved within the group and by the group.
6. Because the need to arrive at a task decision is all-important in the eyes of the leader, needs of individual members are considered less important.	6. With help and encouragement from the leader, the members come to realize that the needs, feelings, and purposes of all members should be met so that an awareness of being a group forms.

ACTION TIP 11: USE BRAINSTORMING TO GENERATE CREATIVE IDEAS

The term "brainstorming" is sometimes used to mean any kind of creative thinking. But that misuses the word. Brainstorming is a specific technique using explicit rules for idea generation and development. This approach requires a communication climate in which the free expression of all kinds of ideas is valued and encouraged—no matter how offbeat or bizarre they may seem. Brainstorming uses four underlying beliefs:

1. *No idea may be criticized.* No comments; no grunts or groans; no thumbs-down gestures. Just let it come out and be recorded.
2. *No idea is too wild.*
3. *Quantity* of ideas generated is important. Push to get as many ideas, as possible, without regard to whether they make any sense at this point.
4. *Hitchhiking is important.* Participants should add to or amplify ideas suggested by others.

The climate set by the meeting leader can promote or hamper the use of brainstorming. A climate that encourages humor and informality works best. Many leaders like to post the four principles where everyone can refer to them.

ACTION TIP 12: ASSIGN SPECIFIC FOLLOW-UP ACTIONS

Be sure that group members have their "marching orders." A brilliant decision is of no value if it isn't implemented, and the people who made the decision are the best ones to direct implementation.

Follow-up assignments typically include informing people of the new action, training people in implementation, creating forms or written instructions for implementing it, and communicating the action and its timing to key people.

A FINAL THOUGHT

Meetings hold the potential for generating good ideas if they are handled well. A meeting aimed at generating E-Plus ideas will be more successful if you apply the tips presented in this chapter. Now, let's try on the behaviors and see what great ideas we can generate.

Activity: Plan and Run a Brainstorming (E-Plus) Meeting

Select one of the following organizations and run an E-Plus meeting. Come up with at least two ideas for each of the VISPAC categories.

1. The company you are currently working in. (After the meeting, prepare a memo describing your ideas and present it to your boss.)
2. Your university bookstore.
3. A restaurant you frequently patronize.
4. Your favorite supermarket.
5. A video store.
6. An upscale clothing shop (boutique).

Try your skills at setting a climate, articulating the topic, running the meeting, capturing ideas, and planning the follow-up necessary to implement ideas your group produces.

If you do not work in an organization or cannot get permission to run the meeting in the company, use your class as the "company" and develop E-Plus ideas for making the students (customers) more satisfied with the course.

Index